SHIFTING SANDS

GULF COUNTRIES, BRICS, AND THE NEW WORLD ORDER

GEW INTELLIGENCE UNIT

GLOBAL EAST-WEST FOR RESEARCH & STUDIES

CONTENTS

MOTIVATION AND OBJECTIVES OF THE BOOK

— • —

The global order is transforming significantly, with shifting power dynamics and emerging multilateral alliances. One such alliance that has gained momentum in recent years is the BRICS+ consortium. Comprising the five BRICS countries (Brazil, Russia, India, China, South Africa) and other countries, the BRICS+ consortium is steadily establishing itself as a major force in the global economy. This book aims to delve deeper into the economic perspectives and potential of the BRICS+ consortium, shedding light on various aspects of its influence and impact.

One major aspect this book will explore is the economic growth and development patterns within the BRICS+ consortium. Despite varying levels of development and different economic models, these countries collectively represent a significant share of the world's population and GDP. By conducting a comparative analysis of their economic policies, structural reforms, and growth strategies, this book aims to provide insights into the future trajectory of the consortium.

With its vast natural resources and agricultural potential, Brazil has been focusing on diversifying its economy, reducing income inequality, and fostering innovation. As a major oil and gas producer, Russia has been working on enhancing its manufacturing capabilities and promoting technological advancements through research and development. India, with its expanding middle class and robust service industry, has been emphasising infrastructure development, foreign investment, and sustainable growth. China, the world's second-largest economy, has been transitioning from an export-oriented economy to a consumption-driven model while investing heavily in innovation, renewable energy, and infrastructure domestically and globally. Despite being the smallest economy among the BRICS, South Africa possesses significant mineral resources and has been promoting inclusive growth, sustainable development, and regional integration in Africa.

Additionally, this book will explore the potential challenges and opportunities these countries present as they navigate the complexities of global trade and investment relations. It will examine the impact of trade wars, protectionism, and geopolitical tensions on the economic trajectories of the BRICS+ countries. It will also analyse the role of international institutions such as the World Trade Organisation (WTO) and the International Monetary Fund (IMF) in shaping the global economic landscape and influencing the policies and strategies of the consortium.

Trade and investment relations will be another key focus of this book. Member countries of the BRICS+ consortium have been actively expanding their economic ties with each other and other regions. This book will explore the evolving trade patterns and investment flows, identifying key sectors and highlighting potential areas for further collaboration. It will examine the role of regional trade agreements, such as the Eurasian Economic Union (EAEU) and the African Continental Free Trade Area (AfCFTA), in facilitating trade between the BRICS countries and their respective regions. By analysing the trade dynamics and exploring the role of foreign direct investment, it seeks to uncover the driving forces behind the growing interdependence within the consortium.

Innovation is crucial for sustainable economic growth in today's world. This book will delve into the innovation ecosystems within the BRICS+ consortium, examining their intellectual property rights regimes, research and development capabilities, and strategic initiatives to foster innovation. By showcasing successful innovation case studies and identifying areas for collaboration, this book aims to highlight the consortium's potential to contribute to technological advancements and global innovation networks.

In addition to studying the BRICS+ consortium, this book acknowledges the historical significance and relevance of the Gulf Cooperation Council (GCC). As a significant global energy supplier, the GCC has played a pivotal role in the geopolitics and energy dynamics of the Middle East and beyond. This book will examine the energy resources, production capacities, and energy policies of the GCC, analysing their impact on the global economy.

Furthermore, it will explore the diversification efforts the GCC countries undertake to reduce their dependence on hydrocarbon exports and transition towards sustainable and knowledge-based economies. This transition includes investments in renewable energy, infrastructure development, tourism, and promoting innovation and entrepreneurship.

This book aims to explore the intersecting interests between the BRICS+ consortium and the GCC. Both sides possess unique strengths and complementarities that can be leveraged for mutual benefit. By conducting a comprehensive comparative analysis of the economic, political, and strategic dimensions, this book aims to identify potential areas of collaboration, such as energy cooperation, infrastructure development, and technology transfer. It will explore the potential for joint initiatives that capitalise on the resources and expertise of both entities, ultimately contributing to the sustainable development and prosperity of their member nations.

The geopolitics of the BRICS+ consortium and the GCC also deserve attention. This book aims to analyse the changing global order, power struggles, and realignment of geopolitical alliances. It will examine the potential role of the BRICS+ consortium and the GCC in reshaping the global political landscape, particularly vis-a-vis the United States. It will evaluate the impact of geopolitical shifts on international trade and investment flows, as well as the influence of these alliances on regional stability and security.

Strategic and economic convergence between the BRICS+ consortium and the GCC will be another examination area. This book will explore the two entities' security cooperation, military capabilities, counterterrorism efforts, infrastructure development, and connectivity initiatives. By identifying converging interests and exploring avenues for enhanced cooperation, it seeks to foster a deeper understanding of the potential strategic partnerships that could emerge. Policymakers can benefit from this book's insights and policy recommendations to strengthen ties and bolster regional and global stability.

In conclusion, this book is motivated by the shifting power dynamics in the global order and the growing significance of the BRICS+ consortium and the GCC. By offering an in-depth analysis of their economic perspectives, trade and investment relations, innovation capacities, geopolitical implications, and strategic convergence, this book aims to comprehensively understand the emerging trends, potentials, and challenges for the global community. It strives to illuminate pathways for collaboration, cooperation, and sustainable development in a rapidly transforming world.

INTRODUCTION

— • —

The Rise of the Rest: Shifting Power Dynamics in the Global Order

The world order is undergoing significant transformations, shaped by the rise of new power players and evolving geopolitical dynamics. Western nations have dominated global affairs for centuries, dictating the course of international relations and shaping the global economic system. However, in recent decades, we have witnessed the emergence of new actors challenging this Western-centric order.

The Significance of the BRICS+ Consortium

The BRICS+ consortium, comprising Brazil, Russia, India, China, South Africa, and other significant regional powers, has emerged as a formidable force in the global arena. This consortium is reshaping the global balance of power, contributing to a more multipolar world order. Each member of the BRICS+ consortium brings unique strengths and characteristics to the table, creating a diverse and complementary coalition.

Brazil, the largest economy in South America, possesses vast natural resources, including the Amazon rainforest and a wealth of mineral reserves. Its robust agricultural sector, fuelled by advanced agribusiness practises, not only serves domestic needs but also satisfies a significant portion of global food demand. Brazil's rapidly growing middle class has provided a substantial market for goods and services, driving economic growth and attracting foreign investment.

Russia, spanning across Eurasia, is the world's largest country. Its expansive landmass not only houses diverse ecosystems and natural resources but also extends geopolitical influence over Europe and Asia. Russia has become a key player in global energy markets, rich in energy resources, including oil, natural gas, and other minerals. Despite its economic dependence on energy exports, Russia has taken steps toward diversification, focusing on high-tech manufacturing, aerospace engineering, and nuclear technology sectors.

India, with its booming population of over 1.3 billion people, offers a massive market for goods and services. Its younger population and thriving information technology sector have positioned India as a global hub for innovation and entrepreneurship. Indian software engineers, entrepreneurs, and startups have left a remarkable imprint on the world, providing cutting-edge technological solutions and boosting the digital economy. As a result, India's presence in the global tech industry and its increasing influence in international organisations have been steadily rising.

China, the world's most populous country and second-largest economy has transformed into a global economic powerhouse. Its rapid industrialisation, embracing of technological innovation, and massive infrastructure projects, such as the Belt and Road Initiative, have propelled its rise globally. China's manufacturing capabilities, production scale, and growing consumer market make it an indispensable player in the global supply chain. Moreover, its leadership in artificial intelligence, renewable energy, and emerging technologies positions China as a key influencer in shaping the future of various industries.

South Africa, the consortium's sole representative of the African continent, adds regional perspectives and resources. South Africa has established itself as a mining powerhouse with its vast mineral wealth, including gold, diamonds, platinum, and others. Furthermore, its financial sector, well-developed infrastructure, and tourism industry contribute to the country's economic strength within the consortium.

These diverse economies have fostered mutually beneficial relationships within the consortium, driving economic growth, fostering technological advancements, and furthering regional integration. Through strengthened trade ties, increased investment flows, and joint initiatives, the BRICS+ countries have gradually reduced their dependence on the Western-dominated global economic system, carving out their own path to prosperity.

The Gulf Cooperation Council: A Historical Perspective

The Gulf Cooperation Council (GCC), comprising Saudi Arabia, Bahrain, Kuwait, Oman, Qatar, and the United Arab Emirates, is a regional force with immense economic and strategic significance. Geographically positioned amidst vital international trade routes, the GCC countries have been historically connected to global trade and cultural exchanges.

The discovery of vast oil reserves in the Gulf region during the 20th century transformed these nations from predominantly agrarian societies into global energy powerhouses. The plentiful oil revenues the Gulf nations generated fuelled their own economic development and impacted the global energy landscape. Their ability to control and influence oil production and prices endowed them with substantial economic, political, and strategic leverage on the world stage.

Over the years, the GCC countries have effectively utilised their oil wealth to invest in infrastructure, education, healthcare, and economic diversification. They have created thriving business hubs, such as Dubai and Bahrain, attracting multinational corporations, entrepreneurs, and skilled professionals worldwide. This influx of talent and investment has enhanced the Gulf region's capacity to innovate, develop new technologies, and create knowledge-based economies.

In recent years, the GCC countries have actively pursued ambitious economic diversification strategies to reduce their dependency on oil. Recognising the need to transition to sustainable and knowledge-based economies, they have focused on finance, tourism, logistics, information technology, and renewable energy sectors. These strategic initiatives aim to create employment opportunities for their growing populations, foster innovation, and attract foreign investments.

The GCC's geographic location at the crossroads of Europe, Asia, and Africa has further bolstered its role as a vital transportation and logistics hub. Its world-class airports, extensive seaports, and efficient logistics infrastructure facilitate the movement of goods and services, enabling global trade and connectivity. The GCC's ability to connect and serve as a gateway to various regions has elevated its economic significance and enhanced its potential as an influential player in shaping global trade.

Motivation and Objectives of the Book

This book aims to explore the intersection between the BRICS+ consortium and the Gulf Cooperation Council, highlighting the economic, geopolitical, and strategic implications of their collaboration. By examining the converging interests of these two infuential entities, we seek to provide insight into the potential opportunities and challenges arising from their partnership. Furthermore, the book aims to shed light on the implications of this collaboration for the evolving global order and the existing power dynamics.

Through comprehensive research, analysis, and in-depth case studies, we hope to offer policymakers, scholars, and readers a holistic understanding of the evolving global order and the role of the BRICS+ consortium and the Gulf Cooperation Council within it. By delving into the economic, geopolitical, and strategic aspects, we seek to provide a comprehensive perspective on the implications and future scenarios for these collaborating entities and the global stage as a whole.

As we embark on this exploration, it is crucial to recognise the significance of non-Western powers in shaping the future of global affairs. The rise of the BRICS+ consortium and the continued prominence of the Gulf Cooperation Council exemplify the diversification and redistribution of power in the global arena. By examining their collaboration and its implications, we can gain valuable insights into the changing dynamics of international relations and the emergence of new power centres that will shape the course of the global order.

1

THE RISE OF THE REST: SHIFTING POWER DYNAMICS IN THE GLOBAL ORDER

— ✦ —

I n the past few decades, the world has witnessed a significant shift in the global order. Traditionally dominated by Western powers, the emergence of new economic and political players has disrupted the status quo and introduced a new era of power dynamics. This chapter explores the rise of the rest, a term coined by political scientist Fareed Zakaria, and the implications it has for the global order.

The rise of the rest refers to the increasing economic and political influence of non-Western countries on the global stage. This phenomenon can be attributed to several factors, including the rapid economic growth of emerging economies, advancements in technology and connectivity, and shifting geopolitical alignments. Countries such as China, India, Brazil, Russia, and South Africa, collectively known as the BRICS countries, have played a crucial role in this transformation.

One of the key drivers of the rise of the rest is economic growth. The BRICS economies, in particular, have experienced remarkable expansion, contributing to a significant increase in their global economic power. China, as the most prominent member of the BRICS, has witnessed an unprecedented economic transformation, becoming the world's second-largest economy. Its rise as a manufacturing powerhouse and global trading partner has had ripple effects across the globe.

China's economic growth has been fuelled by a series of reforms initiated in the late 1970s under the leadership of Deng Xiaoping. These reforms, including the opening up of the Chinese market, the establishment of Special Economic Zones, and the emphasis on export-oriented manufacturing, have propelled the country's economy to new heights. China's integration into the global economy through trade and investments has significantly contributed to its rise as a major player.

Likewise, India has emerged as a major player in the global economy. With a vast consumer market, a thriving technology sector, and a young demographic, India has become an attractive destination for foreign investments. Its vibrant startup ecosystem and skilled workforce have positioned the country as an innovation hub and a driver of digital transformation. India's economic growth, powered by sectors such as information technology, pharmaceuticals, and services, has brought it to the forefront of global economic discussions.

Brazil, with its rich natural resources and agricultural prowess, has transformed into a key player in global food production and energy markets. The country's abundant land and favourable climate conditions have made it an agricultural powerhouse, making significant contributions to global food security. Additionally, Brazil's domestic oil production and biofuel industry have enabled it to enhance its energy security and establish itself as a major player in the global energy sector.

Russia, with its vast energy reserves, geopolitical influence, and military capabilities, has reasserted itself as a major power player on the world stage. Despite economic challenges and geopolitical tensions, Russia's natural resource wealth, especially in the form of oil and gas, has provided the country with significant leverage in international affairs. Furthermore, Russia's military capabilities and strategic positioning give it a voice in shaping the security dynamics of various regions.

South Africa, on the other hand, as an influential voice for the African continent, has been driving regional integration efforts and expanding its economic ties with other emerging economies. As one of Africa's leading economies, South Africa has established itself as a gateway for investment into the African continent. Its membership in organisations such as the African Union and the Southern African Development Community has helped promote regional cooperation and enhance its influence.

Another factor contributing to the shifting power dynamics is the rise of regional alliances and organisations. The BRICS countries, along with other emerging economies, have formed alliances and collaborations that promote closer economic, political, and strategic cooperation. The New Development Bank, established by the BRICS, aims to provide alternative funding mechanisms for infrastructure projects in developing countries, challenging the dominance of Western-led institutions such as the World Bank and the International Monetary Fund.

Moreover, regional alliances like the African Union, the Eurasian Economic Union, and the Association of Southeast Asian Nations (ASEAN) are gaining momentum as platforms for enhancing regional integration, promoting economic growth, and addressing shared challenges. These collaborations not only strengthen the collective bargaining power of emerging economies but also offer alternative avenues for decision-making and global governance.

The rise of the rest poses both opportunities and challenges to the existing global order. Traditional Western powers may feel threatened by the increasing influence and assertiveness of these emerging economies, leading to potential tensions and competition. The reconfiguration of power dynamics can strain existing institutions and norms, demanding a recalibration of international relations.

Furthermore, the rise of the rest brings new perspectives, interests, and priorities to global challenges such as climate change, poverty reduction, or security. Cooperation among nations becomes increasingly essential to tackle these pressing issues effectively. The formation of the BRICS Climate Change Cooperation Fund, for example, demonstrates the commitment of emerging economies to contribute to global climate action by supporting sustainable development projects and green technology transfer.

The rise of the rest also offers opportunities for collaboration and cooperation. As power becomes more distributed, countries have the chance to work together on shared interests and challenges. The convergence of interests between the BRICS countries and the Gulf Cooperation Council (GCC) countries, for example, offers potential avenues for economic, technological, and strategic cooperation. The GCC countries, endowed with vast hydrocarbon resources and seeking economic diversification, can benefit from partnering with the BRICS economies to leverage their technology, market access, and investment capabilities.

By leveraging their respective strengths and resources, these emerging players can shape the global order in a way that reflects the diverse aspirations and interests of different regions. The rise of the rest signifies a fundamental shift in power dynamics within the global order. While this shift brings both challenges and opportunities, it requires a nuanced understanding and a willingness to engage in collaborative and inclusive approaches to global governance.

In conclusion, the rise of the rest has reshaped the global order and introduced a more multipolar world. The remarkable economic growth of emerging economies, coupled with the formation of regional alliances, challenges the Western-dominated international system. However, as power becomes more distributed, opportunities for collaboration and cooperation between traditional powers and emerging players emerge. Adapting to the shifting power dynamics and embracing a more inclusive and multipolar approach to global governance will be key in addressing global challenges and ensuring a peaceful and prosperous future for all nations.

2

THE SIGNIFICANCE OF THE **BRICS+** CONSORTIUM

— • —

The BRICS+ consortium, originally formed as BRICS (Brazil, Russia, India, China, and South Africa), has expanded its membership to include other influential emerging economies such as Mexico, Indonesia, Turkey, and other notable countries. This consortium holds immense importance in the current global order, signifying a transformative shift in power dynamics and challenging the traditional dominance of Western powers. Let us delve deeper into the multifaceted significance of the BRICS+ consortium.

Firstly, the consortium holds substantial economic significance. The combined economic strength of the member countries is staggering, representing over 40% of the world's population, around 25% of global GDP, and a significant share of global trade and investment flows. These countries have shown remarkable economic growth rates and have become attractive investment destinations for both developed and developing nations. With their rapidly growing economies and increasing influence in global financial institutions, the BRICS+ countries aim to create alternative financial arrangements that disrupt the long-standing Western-dominated institutions. This pursuit challenges the existing economic order and presents a more inclusive approach to global economic governance.

Moreover, the BRICS+ consortium serves as a platform for South-South cooperation and development. The member countries recognise the importance of collaboration to address shared challenges and foster inclusive growth. Through trade and investment partnerships, technology transfers, and capacity-building efforts, the consortium facilitates the exchange of knowledge, resources, and experiences among member countries. This collaboration promotes sustainable development practises, strengthens social welfare systems, and drives innovation. Consequently, the BRICS+ consortium has the potential to exert significant influence on global development agendas, advocating for the interests and aspirations of emerging economies.

Additionally, the BRICS+ consortium plays a crucial role in promoting multipolarity in global politics. It provides an alternative voice to the traditional Western powers and challenges their unilateralism. By coordinating their positions on key global issues, such as climate change, trade, and geopolitical conflicts, the member countries leverage their collective influence in global decision-making processes. This concerted effort to foster a more equitable and representative global governance system resonates with the aspirations of developing countries worldwide. It also encourages dialogue and cooperation among different regions and promotes a more balanced global order.

Furthermore, the BRICS+ consortium holds tremendous potential for fostering innovation and technological advancements. Many member countries have recognised the importance of investing in research and development, promoting entrepreneurship, and building robust innovation ecosystems. By collaborating and sharing knowledge, the consortium enables member countries to leverage their collective resources and expertise in various technological domains, such as artificial intelligence (AI), renewable energy, and digital connectivity. This commitment to innovation not only drives economic diversification and productivity gains but also contributes to sustainable development within member countries and beyond.

Importantly, the BRICS+ consortium also aims to strengthen regional alliances and promote multilateralism. The consortium recognises that issues and challenges faced by one member country often have ripple effects on the others. By fostering regional cooperation through platforms such as the BRICS New Development Bank and the Asia-Pacific Economic Cooperation (APEC), the consortium provides financial and technical support for infrastructure development, energy cooperation, and other mutually beneficial projects. These initiatives strengthen regional stability, promote sustainable resource management, and contribute to the emergence of a more interconnected and resilient global order.

In conclusion, the BRICS+ consortium signifies the rise of emerging economies as potent forces in the global order. Its expansion beyond the original BRICS countries speaks to the growing influence and relevance of these dynamic economies. By strategically aligning their economic and political interests, the member countries aim to foster economic growth, promote South-South cooperation, advocate for multipolarity, and drive technological advancements. The significance of the BRICS+ consortium lies in its potential to reshape the global economic and political landscape by challenging the traditional Western dominance and providing a platform for emerging economies to assert their influence and contribute to global decision-making processes. This transformative coalition fosters economic empowerment, regional stability, and sustainable development, paving the way for a more balanced and inclusive global order.

3

THE GULF COOPERATION COUNCIL: A HISTORICAL PERSPECTIVE

— • —

The Gulf Cooperation Council: A Historical Perspective

The Gulf Cooperation Council (GCC), composed of Bahrain, Kuwait, Oman, Qatar, Saudi Arabia, and the United Arab Emirates (UAE), is a regional organisation that has played a pivotal role in shaping the Gulf region over the years. Established in 1981, the GCC has sought to enhance cooperation and integration among its member states, primarily focusing on economic and security matters.

To truly understand the historical roots of the GCC, one must delve into the 1960s, a period characterised by heightened regional awareness and the recognition of the need for unity and collaboration among Gulf countries. In the aftermath of British decolonisation efforts, these nations faced various challenges, including territorial disputes, regional security threats, and economic vulnerabilities. The emergence of the GCC was a response to these challenges; member states realised that by working together, they could effectively address shared concerns and safeguard their collective interests.

The Arab-Israeli conflict, the Iranian Revolution of 1979, and the Iran-Iraq war further accelerated the push for Gulf unity. These events highlighted the vulnerability of individual Gulf nations and underscored the importance of standing together to counter external threats and improve regional stability.

In May 1981, leaders from Bahrain, Kuwait, Oman, Qatar, Saudi Arabia, and the UAE displayed their commitment to collaboration by signing the Declaration of the Gulf

Cooperation Council in Abu Dhabi. This landmark agreement laid the foundation for the organisation and set forth its primary objectives: promoting economic integration and fostering closer political cooperation among member countries.

Over the years, the GCC has emerged as a leading force in the region, significantly shaping regional dynamics and fostering stability in the Gulf. With its comprehensive approach, the organisation has taken on numerous initiatives and agreements to promote integration.

One notable achievement of the GCC has been establishing a common market. In 2008, member states eliminated most trade barriers among themselves, allowing for the free movement of goods, services, and capital within the GCC. This has boosted intra-regional trade and investment, contributing to economic growth and diversification. The common market has also attracted foreign investment and facilitated the creation of a more business-friendly environment, stimulating innovation and entrepreneurship in the Gulf region.

In addition to the common market, the GCC has worked toward creating a customs union, which was launched in 2015. Member countries harmonise their customs policies through this initiative and implement a common external tariff, further facilitating trade and investment flows. The customs union has streamlined logistical processes, reduced trade costs, and enhanced market access for businesses operating within the GCC.

The GCC's efforts extend beyond economic integration. The organisation has also prioritised coordinating defence and security policies to enhance regional stability. The Peninsula Shield Force, initiated in 1984, serves as a joint defence force that can be deployed to member states facing security threats. This mechanism has played a crucial role in maintaining the collective security of the Gulf region. Additionally, the GCC has undertaken various initiatives to combat terrorism, promote counterterrorism cooperation, and share intelligence and best practices among member states.

The GCC's commitment to deeper economic integration and cooperation is exemplified by establishing the Gulf Monetary Council in 2010. This council was tasked with introducing a common currency, aiming to enhance monetary stability and facilitate further economic integration among member countries. Although the goal of a common currency has faced challenges and has yet to be fully realised, the establishment of the Gulf Monetary Council highlights the GCC's determination to strengthen economic ties within the organisation.

Diplomacy has also been a significant aspect of the GCC's agenda. The organisation has actively engaged in mediating conflicts and supporting regional peace initiatives. Notably, during the 2017 Qatar crisis, which saw diplomatic tensions between Qatar and several neighbouring countries, the GCC played a vital role in facilitating dialogue and reconciliation, thereby highlighting its commitment to resolving disputes and maintaining regional cohesion. The GCC's diplomacy efforts have extended beyond the Gulf region, with engagements in regional forums and international platforms to promote dialogue, cooperation, and peaceful resolutions.

The GCC has actively pursued partnerships and collaborations with other regional and international organisations to expand its reach and influence beyond the Gulf. It has engaged with the United Nations, the Arab League, and the Organisation of Islamic Cooperation, among others, to address common challenges on a broader scale. These partnerships have allowed the GCC to amplify its influence and effectively address issues such as terrorism, extremism, and environmental sustainability. The organisation has also engaged in numerous agreements and dialogues with countries outside the Gulf region, fostering economic, political, and cultural ties.

However, the GCC has not been immune to internal tensions and disagreements that have sometimes strained its unity. Differences in political and economic ideologies among member states have presented challenges in the organisation's decision-making process and hindered the pace of integration. Furthermore, the outbreak of the Arab Spring uprisings in 2011 tested the GCC's ability to respond collectively to regional crises. While the GCC remained united in its opposition to some aspects of the uprisings, it faced internal divisions over intervention strategies, political ideologies, and external alliances.

Nevertheless, the GCC has proven its resilience and adaptability, which has enabled it to navigate challenging periods while remaining a significant regional actor. The organisation has continuously adjusted its strategies and initiatives to address emerging challenges and opportunities. In recent years, combating terrorism, countering extremism, and addressing climate change and environmental issues have become key focus areas for the GCC, underscoring its commitment to regional stability and sustainability. The GCC has actively pursued renewable energy initiatives, invested in sustainable infrastructure, and promoted environmental conservation efforts to ensure a greener and more sustainable Gulf region.

In conclusion, the Gulf Cooperation Council's historical journey has shaped the Gulf region and positioned it as a key player internationally. The GCC continues to strengthen regional stability, solidarity, and prosperity through its ongoing efforts to deepen economic integration, foster political cooperation, address security challenges, promote diplomacy, and engage with international partners. The organisation's adaptability and commitment to collective action in the face of evolving regional and international dynamics underscore its significance as a symbol of unity and cooperation in the Gulf.

4

THE BRICS+ CONSORTIUM: ECONOMIC PERSPECTIVES

— · —

T he BRICS+ consortium, consisting of the five original BRICS countries (Brazil, Russia, India, China, and South Africa) and additional partner countries, has emerged as a significant force in the global economy. This chapter delves into the economic perspectives of the BRICS+ consortium, examining various aspects such as economic growth and development patterns, trade and investment relations, innovation and technological advancements, and the role of BRICS+ in addressing global economic challenges.

Economic Growth and Development Patterns Among BRICS+ Countries

The BRICS+ countries collectively represent a significant share of global GDP, population, and natural resources. Over the past few decades, these nations have witnessed substantial economic growth and development. However, their growth patterns vary, reflecting diverse economic structures.

China, the largest economy among the BRICS+ countries, has adopted a model driven by exports, manufacturing, and infrastructure development. Its rapid industrialisation and export-oriented policies have resulted in robust GDP growth. China's manufacturing sector has flourished, propelled by its skilled workforce, strong logistical networks, and government support for research and development.

With its vast domestic market, India has seen a surge in consumption-led growth. The country has embraced its service sector, particularly information technology and business process outsourcing. Additionally, India has implemented initiatives such as Make in

India and Digital India to encourage manufacturing and inclusive digital transformation.

Brazil, known for its rich natural resources and agricultural prowess, has expanded its export markets by diversifying its industrial base and focusing on sectors such as aerospace, renewable energy, and biofuels. Brazil has also made significant progress in addressing income inequality and poverty through social welfare programmes.

Russia, with its extensive reserves of oil, natural gas, and minerals, has relied heavily on energy exports. However, it has recognised the need to diversify its economy, emphasising technology development, innovation, and manufacturing. Russia has also prioritised the modernisation of its infrastructure and the promotion of entrepreneurship.

Although facing structural challenges, South Africa has made efforts to promote sustainable economic growth. The country has prioritised mining, tourism, financial services, and renewable energy sectors. South Africa also focuses on fostering entrepreneurship and improving education and skills development.

Trade and Investment Relations within BRICS+ and with the Gulf Countries

Trade and investment play a vital role in the economic dynamics of the BRICS+ countries. The intra-BRICS+ trade relations have flourished over the years, with partnerships spanning diverse sectors, such as manufacturing, technology, agriculture, and energy.

China, as the manufacturing powerhouse, has been a major trading partner for other BRICS+ nations, supplying machinery, electronics, and consumer goods while importing raw materials and agricultural products. China has also increased its investments in other BRICS+ countries to spur economic growth and forge closer trade ties.

India's expanding consumer market has attracted investments from other BRICS+ countries, promoting joint ventures, technology transfers, and knowledge sharing. India has also focused on strengthening trade relations with its BRICS+ counterparts by signing bilateral trade agreements and seeking to reduce trade barriers.

Brazil's agricultural products, including soybeans, meat, and coffee, have found substantial markets within the BRICS+ consortium. Additionally, Brazil has made efforts to boost trade and investment relations with other BRICS+ countries by facilitating business delegation exchanges, promoting cultural exchanges, and enhancing connectivity through infrastructure projects.

Russia's vast energy resources have forged strong economic ties within the BRICS+ consortium. It has supplied oil, natural gas, and other energy products to meet the growing demands of its partners. Furthermore, Russia has actively sought to enhance technological cooperation and attract investments in various sectors such as aerospace, healthcare, and digital innovation.

With its abundant mineral resources, South Africa has focused on expanding trade relations with other BRICS+ nations. The country exports minerals, precious metals, and agricultural products while importing machinery, equipment, and manufactured goods. South Africa also seeks to foster stronger ties with the Gulf Cooperation Council (GCC) countries, promoting trade and investment opportunities in sectors such as mining, energy, tourism, and infrastructure development.

Innovation and Technological Advancements in BRICS+ Economies

Innovation and technology are crucial drivers of economic growth and competitiveness. Recognising this, the BRICS+ countries have prioritised fostering innovation by investing in research and development, promoting entrepreneurship, and upgrading their technological capabilities.

China, for instance, has launched the "Made in China 2025" strategy, focusing on high-tech industries such as aerospace, biotechnology, artificial intelligence, and robotics. This ambitious plan aims to transform China into a global leader in advanced technologies and enhance the quality and value of its products.

India has been a hub for information technology and software development, becoming a major global IT services market player. The country has also launched initiatives like the Start-up India and Digital India campaigns to encourage entrepreneurship, digital innovation, and the adoption of emerging technologies such as blockchain and the Internet of Things (IoT).

Brazil has made significant progress in biofuels and renewable energy technologies, capitalising on its vast agricultural resources and aiming to reduce its carbon footprint. The country has also focused on fostering innovation in sectors such as aerospace, pharmaceuticals, and agribusiness, pushing for greater research and development collaboration.

Russia has invested in space technology, nuclear energy, and advanced manufacturing. The country's space agency, Roscosmos, has been at the forefront of space exploration while its nuclear industry has expanded globally. Russia has also supported research and development in various fields, including artificial intelligence, biotechnology, and information technology.

South Africa, known for its mining sector, has made strides in developing environmental technologies to address sustainability challenges. The country has also invested in digital innovation and advanced manufacturing to enhance its competitiveness in global markets. South Africa has emphasised research and development collaboration, technology transfers, and skills development to drive innovation.

The BRICS+ consortium has fostered collaboration among its member countries by establishing research institutions and joint projects. Platforms such as the BRICS Innovation Cooperation Action Plan have facilitated knowledge sharing, technology transfers, and joint development of innovative solutions to common challenges. Moreover, the consortium encourages cooperation with external partners, international organisations, and academia to harness collective expertise and accelerate technological advancements.

Role of BRICS+ in Addressing Global Economic Challenges

The global economic landscape faces numerous challenges, including economic inequality, climate change, digital transformation, and sustainable development. The BRICS+ consortium recognises its role in addressing these challenges and strives to contribute solutions.

As emerging economies, the BRICS+ countries are vested in fostering inclusive growth, reducing poverty, and improving socio-economic indicators. They prioritise social welfare systems, healthcare, education, and skills development to uplift their population and bridge inequalities. Programmes like China's poverty alleviation campaigns and India's initiatives for financial inclusion and rural development have shown some positive results.

Additionally, the BRICS+ consortium acknowledges the importance of sustainable development and has shown commitment to climate mitigation and environmental conservation efforts. These countries have implemented various policies and initiatives to promote renewable energy, green industries, sustainable urban development, and environmental protection. Efforts such as China's promotion of electric vehicles, India's renewable energy targets, Brazil's initiatives to combat deforestation, Russia's commitment to the Paris Agreement, and South Africa's transition to a low-carbon economy demonstrate their commitment to addressing climate change and promoting sustainable development.

The BRICS+ countries also recognise the need to adapt to the ongoing digital transformation and harness the opportunities presented by the Fourth Industrial Revolution. They have prioritised investments in digital infrastructure, connectivity, and digital skills development. Initiatives such as China's Belt and Road Initiative, India's Digital India campaign, Brazil's digital transformation strategy, Russia's digital economy programme, and South Africa's e-commerce support initiatives aim to enhance digital connectivity, promote e-commerce, and foster digital innovation.

Furthermore, the BRICS+ countries actively shape the global economic governance framework. They advocate for a more inclusive and representative international financial system, calling for reforms in institutions such as the International Monetary Fund (IMF) and the World Bank. The creation of the BRICS New Development Bank and the Contingent Reserve Arrangement is an example of their efforts to establish alternative financial institutions that promote development and provide stability during global economic uncertainty.

The BRICS+ consortium also promotes South-South cooperation and collaboration with other developing countries, particularly through initiatives such as the BRICS-Africa Partnership, the BRICS Plus outreach, and the Asia-Africa Growth Corridor. They recognise the importance of mutual support and solidarity among developing nations in achieving sustainable and inclusive development.

In conclusion, the BRICS+ consortium, comprised of Brazil, Russia, India, China, South Africa, and additional partner countries, has emerged as a significant force in the global economy. These countries have witnessed substantial economic growth and development driven by diverse economic structures and strategies. Trade and investment relations within the consortium have flourished, along with collaborations to foster innovation and technological advancements. The BRICS+ countries also recognise their role in addressing global economic challenges through inclusive growth, sustainable development, and digital transformation. Through their collective efforts, the BRICS+ consortium aims to shape the global economic landscape and contribute to a more equitable and sustainable future.

5

ECONOMIC GROWTH AND DEVELOPMENT PATTERNS AMONG BRICS+ COUNTRIES

— • —

Economic Growth and Development Patterns Among BRICS+ Countries

The BRICS+ consortium comprises emerging economies that have experienced significant economic growth and development over the past few decades. This chapter explores the various patterns and trends observed among these countries regarding their economic performance, delving deeper into the factors driving their success.

One common thread among BRICS+ countries is their ability to achieve high levels of economic growth. China, particularly, has been the driving force behind this growth, with its rapid industrialisation and export-oriented policies. The country's success can be attributed to its strategic focus on infrastructure development, technological advancements, and competitive manufacturing sectors. China's massive investments in transport systems, energy networks, and digital infrastructure have facilitated trade, enhanced connectivity, and boosted productivity. Moreover, the coordinated efforts between the government and private sector have fostered innovation, leading to the rise of tech giants like Alibaba and Tencent.

Another prominent member of the BRICS+ consortium, India, has also experienced remarkable economic growth. Its success can be attributed to its favourable demographic trends, with a young and aspiring population driving consumption and entrepreneurship. India's vibrant services sector, including information technology, business process outsourcing, and financial services, has played a crucial role in its economic transformation. India's IT sector has become a global leader, providing technology solutions and services to diverse industries worldwide. Furthermore, India's substantial investment in research and development has contributed to advancements in pharmaceuticals, biotechnology, and space technology, positioning the country as a hub for innovation in these sectors.

Brazil, Russia, and South Africa have faced unique challenges in their economic growth trajectories. Brazil has often grappled with political uncertainties and structural issues, yet it has built a diverse economy supported by its agricultural, manufacturing, and services sectors. The country is the world's largest exporter of beef, poultry, and soybeans, and it has successfully developed a globally competitive aerospace industry. Furthermore, Brazil's services sector, particularly tourism and creative industries, has been instrumental in generating employment and driving economic growth. However, to sustain long-term growth, Brazil must address issues such as income inequality, corruption, and underinvestment in education and infrastructure.

Endowed with abundant natural resources, particularly oil and gas, Russia has relied heavily on these sectors for economic growth. However, this dependence on commodities subjects the country to volatility in global markets. In recent years, Russia has endeavoured to diversify its economy by promoting aerospace, information technology, and advanced manufacturing sectors. The Skolkovo Innovation Centre, for instance, nurtures technology startups and fosters collaboration between research institutions and businesses. Moreover, Russia's increased focus on innovation and research has fuelled technological advancements and scientific breakthroughs in sectors like nuclear technology, space exploration, and robotics.

South Africa, the gateway to Africa's markets, has demonstrated resilience and progress in various sectors. While the country faces socio-economic challenges, it has made significant strides in mining, tourism, manufacturing, and financial services. Recognising the importance of economic inclusivity, South Africa has implemented policies to address inequality and promote small and medium-sized enterprises. Moreover, the country's commitment to renewable energy has placed it at Africa's forefront of renewable energy development. South Africa's advancements in wind and solar energy have helped diversify its energy mix and positioned it as a significant player in the global renewable energy sector.

The development patterns among BRICS+ countries extend beyond their economic growth rates. These nations have recognised the importance of building a strong knowledge-based economy and have invested substantially in infrastructure development, human capital, and innovation. They have prioritised education and research, leading to the establishment of world-class universities and research institutions. China's Tsinghua University, for example, is known for its excellence in science and engineering, while India's Indian Institutes of Technology have nurtured generations of top-notch engineering talent. Furthermore, these countries have actively sought foreign direct investment, fostered innovation ecosystems, and encouraged the growth of entrepreneurship to drive technological advancements.

Another notable aspect is the diversification of economies among the BRICS+ countries. Many of these nations have acknowledged the risks of relying on a single sector or commodity and have implemented policies to encourage diversification. By promoting industries such as technology, renewable energy, healthcare, and advanced manufacturing, these countries aim to ensure long-term economic stability and reduce vulnerabilities to external shocks. Brazil's government, for instance, has implemented incentives to attract investments in green industries, promoting sustainability and driving economic growth simultaneously.

However, while the BRICS+ countries have enjoyed significant economic growth, challenges remain. Income inequality, poverty, and social disparities persist in many of these nations. Additionally, issues such as corruption, political instabilities, and the need for structural reforms continue to hinder their growth potential. Overcoming these challenges will require sustained efforts to create inclusive policies, promote good governance, and invest in social infrastructure. For example, Brazil needs to address corruption issues and improve governance to facilitate business operations and improve investor confidence.

In conclusion, the BRICS+ countries have displayed impressive economic growth and development patterns over the years. Their success can be attributed to their strategic focus on infrastructure development, human capital, innovation, and diversification of their economies. However, addressing remaining challenges and working towards inclusive growth will be critical for sustainable development and unlocking the full potential of these nations. As their economies continue to evolve, the BRICS+ countries are poised to play an increasingly influential role in shaping global economic dynamics. By fostering collaborative partnerships and leveraging their strengths, these emerging economies are well-positioned to contribute to global economic growth and development in the years to come.

6

TRADE AND INVESTMENT RELATIONS WITHIN BRICS+ AND WITH THE GULF COUNTRIES

— · —

The trade and investment dynamics between the BRICS+ countries (Brazil, Russia, India, China, and South Africa) and the Gulf countries (Saudi Arabia, United Arab Emirates, Qatar, Oman, Bahrain, and Kuwait) have gained significant attention in recent years, given their immense potential for collaboration and economic growth. This chapter aims to provide an in-depth analysis of the patterns, challenges, and potential areas of cooperation within these economic relationships.

Trade and Investment Patterns within BRICS+

The BRICS+ countries have gradually deepened their economic ties, with trade and investment flows becoming increasingly robust. One primary driver of these relationships is resource complementarity. Brazil, for instance, is a major exporter of agricultural products, while Russia possesses abundant reserves of natural resources. Conversely, China is a manufacturing powerhouse, and India is known for its information technology services. Such complementary strengths have facilitated trade diversification and the formation of joint ventures in various sectors.

Trade within the BRICS+ countries has seen significant growth over the years. In 2020, total exports between the BRICS countries reached USD 1.27 trillion, a 2.6% increase from the previous year. China remained the largest trading partner, accounting for around 59.5% of intra-BRICS exports, followed by Russia (15.1%), India (13%), Brazil

(8.7%), and South Africa (3.7%). These figures indicate the substantial level of trade integration within the consortium, driven by their combined population of 3.6 billion people and a GDP of approximately USD 18.8 trillion.

The manufacturing industry has witnessed substantial growth within the BRICS+ consortium. China's manufacturing sector, in particular, has developed close supply chains with the other member countries. This close integration has resulted in a significant level of intra-BRICS trade in manufacturing goods. For example, machinery and mechanical appliances accounted for 36% of China's exports to Russia in 2020, while electrical machinery and equipment represented 18.4% of China's exports to India.

Additionally, the services sector has played a crucial role in driving economic cooperation among the BRICS+ countries, accounting for a significant share of their GDPs. India's software development and IT services expertise has propelled its services exports to other BRICS countries. Brazil and South Africa have also witnessed growth in their services sectors, particularly in finance, tourism, and business services. Information technology services, finance, and tourism have become key areas of collaboration within the consortium, contributing to economic growth and job creation.

Investment within the BRICS+ consortium has also been essential in fostering economic collaboration. Chinese investments, driven by its Belt and Road Initiative (BRI), have facilitated infrastructure development projects in various BRICS+ countries. These investments have included the construction of transportation networks, energy facilities, and industrial zones. On the other hand, Russian investments have focused on sectors such as energy, natural resources, automotive manufacturing, and financial services in other BRICS+ nations.

Trade and Investment Relations with the Gulf Countries

The Gulf countries, endowed with enormous energy reserves and strategic geographic location, present immense opportunities for trade and investment for the BRICS+ countries. Bilateral trade between the Gulf Cooperation Council (GCC) and the BRICS+ countries has steadily increased in recent years. In 2020, the total trade between the GCC and the BRICS+ countries reached USD 258 billion, a 14% increase compared to 2019.

The Gulf countries' economies rely highly on energy exports, making energy co-operation a cornerstone of their bilateral trade relations with the BRICS+ countries. China, India, and Russia are the largest oil and gas importers from the Gulf region. In 2020, China imported over 262 million metric tons of oil from the Gulf, accounting for approximately 45% of its total oil imports. India is another major importer, relying on the Gulf for 79% of its total oil imports in 2020. Russia, in addition to being a significant energy consumer, has also been actively exploring oil and gas exploration projects and joint ventures with the Gulf countries.

Moreover, the Gulf countries have been keen to diversify their economies beyond oil and gas, exploring investment opportunities within the BRICS+ countries. Qatar, for instance, has invested in Brazil's agricultural sector, aiming to ensure food security for its population. The UAE and Saudi Arabia have focused on infrastructure development projects and technology companies in India. These investments contribute to job creation, technology transfer, and economic diversification in both regions.

Key Areas of Collaboration

To further enhance trade and investment relations between the BRICS+ countries and the Gulf countries, it is crucial to identify and capitalise on key areas of collaboration. Several areas hold immense potential for mutual growth:

1. Energy Cooperation: While energy cooperation is already robust, there are opportunities for joint ventures in renewable energy projects, research and development, and technology transfers. Sharing best practices in energy efficiency and exploring investment opportunities in clean energy infrastructure can foster a more sustainable and resilient energy sector.

2. Infrastructure Development: The BRICS+ nations' expertise in construction, engineering, and logistics can support the Gulf countries' infrastructure projects, including the construction of smart cities, transportation networks, and industrial zones. Collaboration in this area can not only boost trade but also facilitate economic diversification in the Gulf region.

3. Technology Transfers and Knowledge-Sharing: The BRICS+ countries have made

significant strides in information technology, telecommunication, and e-commerce sectors. Sharing best practices, facilitating partnerships between startups and established firms, and promoting joint research and development projects can foster innovation and accelerate digital transformation in the Gulf countries.

4. Agricultural Cooperation: Given the Gulf countries' limited arable land and Brazil's prowess in agriculture, there is potential for greater cooperation in agricultural production, technology transfer, and food security. Brazil can leverage its expertise in tropical agriculture to support the Gulf countries' efforts to enhance agricultural productivity and achieve food self-sufficiency.

Overcoming Challenges

To maximise the potential of trade and investment relations between the BRICS+ countries and the Gulf countries, several challenges need to be addressed:

1. Trade Barriers and Restrictive Regulations: Tariffs, non-tariff barriers, and restrictive regulations can hinder the smooth flow of goods and services. Efforts to reduce trade barriers through regional integration initiatives, such as the African Continental Free Trade Area (AfCFTA) and the ASEAN-led Regional Comprehensive Economic Partnership (RCEP), can create a more favourable business environment.

2. Geopolitical Tensions: Regional geopolitical tensions can disrupt trade and investment flows. Diplomatic engagement, dialogue, and negotiations are essential to mitigating these tensions and maintaining a conducive environment for economic cooperation.

3. Infrastructure Gaps: Infrastructure gaps within the BRICS+ countries and the Gulf countries can hamper trade and investment. Bridging these gaps through investments in transportation, logistics, and digital infrastructure is crucial for facilitating cross-border trade and connectivity.

4. Cultural and Business Differences: Differences in business practises, languages, and cultural norms can pose challenges to effective collaboration. Promoting cultural exchanges, organising business forums, and facilitating business-to-business contacts can help bridge these differences and foster better understanding and cooperation.

Conclusion

Trade and investment relations between the BRICS+ countries and the Gulf countries are poised for further growth and collaboration. The BRICS+ countries, with their diverse strengths and resources, can provide valuable opportunities for the Gulf countries to diversify their economies and enhance their competitiveness. Similarly, the Gulf countries, with their vast oil and gas reserves and strategic location, present immense opportunities for the BRICS+ countries to secure energy resources and explore investment opportunities.

To fully realise the potential of these economic relationships, governments and businesses must work together to overcome challenges and create an enabling environment for trade and investment. This includes reducing trade barriers, facilitating regulatory harmonisation, and promoting investment-friendly policies. It is also crucial to foster dialogue and cooperation on geopolitical issues to ensure the stability of trade and investment flows.

Furthermore, enhancing connectivity and infrastructure development will facilitate the smooth movement of goods, services, and people between the BRICS+ countries and the Gulf countries. Investments in transportation networks, logistics hubs, and digital infrastructure will create efficient supply chains and enhance trade facilitation.

In conclusion, the trade and investment relations between the BRICS+ countries and the Gulf countries hold immense potential for mutual growth and collaboration. By addressing challenges, identifying key areas of cooperation, and creating an enabling environment, these relationships can contribute to economic development, job creation, and sustainable growth for both regions.

7

INNOVATION AND TECHNOLOGICAL ADVANCEMENTS IN BRICS+ ECONOMIES

— ◆ —

Innovation and Technological Advancements in BRICS+ Economies

The BRICS+ consortium, which includes emerging economies such as Brazil, Russia, India, China, and other countries from different regions, has witnessed significant advancements in recent years in terms of innovation and technology. These countries have recognised the importance of innovation in driving economic growth, improving competitiveness, and addressing societal challenges.

One of the key drivers of innovation in the BRICS+ economies is the focus on research and development (R&D) activities. Governments in these countries have been increasing investments in R&D infrastructure, fostering collaboration between academia and industry, and promoting entrepreneurship. This has led to establishing research institutes, technology parks, and incubation centres, providing a conducive environment for innovation and technological advancements.

The Chinese government has implemented various initiatives to foster innovation and technological advancements in China. For instance, the "Made in China 2025" strategy focuses on transforming China from a manufacturing-based economy to an innovation-driven one. This involves focusing on sectors such as artificial intelligence (AI), robotics, biotechnology, and new energy vehicles. Through initiatives like these, China aims to become a global technological powerhouse, driving economic growth and improving the quality of life for its citizens.

Another BRICS nation, India, has made significant strides in innovation and tech-nology. The country has emerged as a hub for software development and IT services, contributing to the global digital transformation. With its large pool of skilled IT profes-sionals and competitive advantage in cost-effective solutions, India has attracted multina-tional companies and startups. Initiatives like "Digital India" have bolstered the adoption of digital technology, leading to the rise of startups in areas such as fintech, e-commerce, logistics, and healthcare. Moreover, the "Startup India" campaign has provided various incentives and support to entrepreneurs, encouraging innovation and entrepreneurship in the country.

Brazil, Russia, and other BRICS+ countries have also invested in innovation and technology to drive economic growth. With its diverse and resource-rich economy, Brazil has been focusing on sectors like biotechnology, renewable energy, and advanced man-ufacturing. The country has set up research programmes, innovation hubs, and tech-nology parks to support startups and attract foreign investment. The government has also launched initiatives like "Science Without Borders," which provides scholarships for Brazilian students and researchers to study abroad, facilitating knowledge exchange and fostering innovation. Similarly, Russia has been investing in its Skolkovo Innovation Centre, which aims to promote cooperation between researchers, entrepreneurs, and corporations, fostering innovation in areas such as energy efficiency, information tech-nology, and pharmaceuticals.

Furthermore, the BRICS+ countries have actively promoted research and develop-ment in sustainable technologies. With a shared commitment to addressing environ-mental challenges, these nations drive innovation in renewable energy sources, clean technologies, and green infrastructure. For example, India has launched the International Solar Alliance, bringing together countries to promote solar energy adoption worldwide. With its abundant natural resources, Brazil has been investing in biofuels and sustainable agriculture. Russia, with its extensive expertise in the energy industry, has been focusing on developing clean energy solutions like wind and nuclear power. By adopting sustain-able technologies, these countries are working towards a cleaner future, creating economic opportunities, and diversifying their energy sources.

In addition to the traditional focus on research and development, innovation in the BRICS+ consortium is also driven by the proliferation of digital technologies. Adopting technologies such as artificial intelligence (AI), blockchain, Internet of Things (IoT), and big data analytics is transforming industries and creating new opportunities. In China, AI technologies are utilised in areas ranging from healthcare and finance to transportation and manufacturing. E-commerce platforms and mobile payment systems have gained immense popularity in countries like China and India, revolutionising how people shop and transact. Similarly, Brazil has seen the rise of AgTech (agricultural technology) startups that leverage IoT and data analytics to improve farming practices and increase efficiency.

The BRICS+ countries have been implementing policies to enhance digital infrastructure and connectivity to support innovation and technological advancements. This involves investments in broadband access, digital literacy programmes, and the development of smart cities. For instance, India's "Smart Cities Mission" envisions the creation of 100 smart cities that utilise technology to improve the quality of life for citizens. China has been investing heavily in building 5G infrastructure to enable faster and more efficient data transmission, supporting the development of smart cities, autonomous vehicles, and Internet of Things applications. By bridging the digital divide within their respective economies, these countries ensure their populations have the necessary skills and resources to participate in the digital economy.

In conclusion, the BRICS+ economies have witnessed remarkable progress in terms of innovation and technological advancements. Through increased investments in research and development, the promotion of digital technologies, and a focus on sustainability, these countries are positioning themselves as leaders in innovation-driven growth. The advancements in innovation and technology within the BRICS+ consortium have the potential to transform their own economies, contribute to global advancements, and reshape the future of the global innovation landscape. These emerging economies increasingly become drivers of innovation and technological progress, presenting new opportunities for business collaboration, cross-border partnerships, and knowledge sharing. As they continue to invest in R&D, foster entrepreneurial ecosystems, and leverage digital technologies, the BRICS+ economies are poised to shape the future of innovation and make substantial contributions to global sustainability, economic development, and societal well-being.

8

ROLE OF **BRICS+** IN ADDRESSING GLOBAL ECONOMIC CHALLENGES

— • —

The role of BRICS+ (Brazil, Russia, India, China, South Africa, and their extended partners) in addressing global economic challenges is of significant importance in shaping the future of the global economy. As emerging economies, the BRICS+ countries have been able to achieve remarkable economic growth and development over the past few decades. Their collective influence and potential to address global economic challenges cannot be ignored.

One of the key ways in which BRICS+ contribute to addressing global economic challenges is through their sheer economic size and market potential. The combined GDP of the BRICS+ countries accounts for a substantial portion of the global economy, and they have a significant influence on global economic trends. Their economic growth and consumption patterns have a considerable impact on global trade, investment, and overall economic stability.

BRICS+ countries have emerged as major contributors to global economic growth. Their economic policies, reforms, and investments have positively influenced global economic dynamics and helped drive global demand. For instance, China's rapid industrialisation and increasing middle-class consumption have played a vital role in sustaining global trade flows. Similarly, India's growing consumer market and digital revolution have created new opportunities for businesses worldwide. Russian energy resources, Brazil's agricultural exports, and South Africa's mineral wealth have also contributed significantly to global economic growth.

Moreover, BRICS+ countries have embarked on ambitious innovation and technological development strategies. They recognise the importance of fostering research and development to stay competitive in today's knowledge-based global economy. These countries have made significant strides in sectors such as information technology, manufacturing, renewable energy, biotechnology, and healthcare.

China, for instance, has become a global leader in e-commerce and telecom equipment manufacturing, thanks to investments in research and development. It is also at the forefront of renewable energy adoption, making significant progress in solar and wind power generation. India has established itself as a global hub for software development and IT services, with its indigenous technology companies gaining prominence on the global stage. Additionally, India has been actively pursuing advancements in healthcare, focusing on affordable and innovative solutions. Russia, known for its aerospace engineering and nuclear energy expertise, has successfully created cutting-edge advancements in aerospace technology and is a significant player in the space industry. Brazil has made remarkable progress in biofuel technology, successfully implementing sustainable solutions like ethanol production from sugarcane, reducing reliance on fossil fuels. South Africa has been investing in research and development to diversify its economy and promote renewable energy sources to address climate change issues.

By embracing innovation and technological advancements, BRICS+ countries are not only boosting their own economies but also contributing to global economic development. Their investments in research and development drive job creation, increase productivity, and enhance competitiveness in the global market. Additionally, these countries actively promote collaborations and partnerships with other nations to share knowledge, foster technological advancements, and address global challenges collectively.

BRICS+ countries also play a crucial role in addressing global economic imbalances and inequality. They recognise that economic growth should be inclusive and aim to reduce poverty, improve living standards, and achieve equitable economic progress. Governments within the BRICS+ bloc have implemented various measures to address income disparities, enhance social welfare programmes, and invest in human capital development.

China's poverty alleviation programme is a prime example of this effort, where millions of people have been lifted out of poverty through targeted measures and investments in education and healthcare. India has implemented initiatives such as the Pradhan Mantri Jan Dhan Yojana, which aimed at financial inclusion and providing bank accounts to the unbanked population. Brazil has implemented Bolsa Família, a conditional cash transfer programme that provides direct financial assistance to vulnerable families. South Africa has made strides in improving access to education, healthcare, and social protection, particularly for disadvantaged communities.

Cooperation among BRICS+ countries in areas such as finance, trade, and development finance is vital to addressing global economic challenges. Initiatives such as the New Development Bank (NDB) and the Contingent Reserve Arrangement (CRA) have been set up to provide financial support, promote infrastructure development, and address specific economic challenges in member countries. These institutions further strengthen the collective voice of BRICS+ countries in global economic governance and decision-making processes, providing alternatives to existing multilateral financial organisations. Through these mechanisms, BRICS+ countries can ensure greater representation for emerging economies and contribute to reshaping the global economic architecture.

In conclusion, the role of BRICS+ in addressing global economic challenges is multifaceted and crucial. These countries, with their economic prowess, innovation, and collaborative efforts, have the potential to shape the future of the global economy. By addressing economic imbalances, promoting innovation, and fostering inclusive growth, BRICS+ countries contribute to sustainable development and help address various global economic challenges. Their collective influence and actions will continue to shape the global economic landscape, providing opportunities for shared prosperity and a more balanced global economic order. The continued collaboration and integration of BRICS+ countries will be instrumental in determining the trajectory of the global economy for years to come.

9

GULF COOPERATION COUNCIL: ENERGY DYNAMICS

— • —

H istory of the GCC as Global Energy Suppliers:

The Gulf Cooperation Council (GCC) has a rich and complex history as a global energy supplier with a profound impact on the world economy. Since the discovery of vast energy reserves in the region in the mid-20th century, the member countries of the GCC have played a pivotal role in shaping global energy markets. These countries, including Saudi Arabia, Kuwait, Bahrain, Qatar, UAE, and Oman, possess significant oil and gas reserves, making them important contributors to global energy supply and security.

Energy Resources and Production Capacities of GCC Countries

The GCC countries collectively possess some of the world's largest energy reserves, mainly oil and gas. Saudi Arabia, the largest GCC member, sits atop the largest proven oil reserves globally and maintains significant production capacities. The kingdom has invested heavily in upstream exploration and production technologies to maximise recovery rates and improve efficiency. Kuwait possesses abundant oil resources, characterised by high-quality crude oil with low sulphur content, making it highly sought after in global markets. Qatar, known for its vast natural gas reserves, has become a leading liquefied natural gas (LNG) exporter and is considered one of the most reliable suppliers worldwide.

The UAE has substantial crude oil reserves and significant investments in advanced extraction technologies and infrastructure development. It has diversified its energy mix by incorporating renewable energy sources like solar power, aiming to reduce its carbon footprint and enhance sustainability. While possessing smaller oil and gas reserves, Bahrain relies on strategic partnerships and refining capabilities. It has focused on expanding its refining capacity and establishing itself as a regional trading hub, contributing to global energy markets. With its significant oil reserves, Oman has also invested in enhancing recovery techniques to sustain production levels and attract foreign investments.

Energy Supply and Demand Dynamics in the Global Market

The GCC countries closely monitor energy supply and demand dynamics in the global market due to their status as major energy suppliers. They analyse market trends, fluctuations in oil prices, and shifts in global energy demand patterns to ascertain the appropriate adjustments to production levels and export strategies. Continuous monitoring and analysis enable these countries to make informed decisions regarding investments, exploration strategies, and production quotas, aligning their production capacities with market needs and ensuring stable revenues and economic growth.

The GCC countries are crucial in mitigating global energy supply risks, given their large-scale energy exports. They maintain spare production capacities, known as swing capacities, ready to be deployed in case of disruptions in global oil supplies. This strategic approach helps stabilise global energy markets and ensures the availability of resources during emergencies, thereby averting potential crises and reducing price volatility.

Understanding the Impact of GCC Energy Policies on the Global Economy

The energy policies the GCC countries pursue yield substantial implications for the global economy, extending far beyond energy markets alone. As leading energy exporters, any changes in their production levels, export strategies, or pricing mechanisms can significantly influence global energy markets, impacting various sectors and economies worldwide.

The decisions the GCC countries make regarding production quotas have a ripple effect on oil prices and supply dynamics. Their coordinated efforts, often in collaboration with other major oil-producing countries like Russia, have sometimes succeeded in stabilising prices amid market fluctuations. However, fluctuations in oil prices can have both positive and negative implications. While lower prices may benefit oil-importing countries, they pose challenges to the economies heavily reliant on oil exports, necessitating diversification efforts.

The GCC countries have recognised the urgency of diversifying their economies beyond oil and gas. They have initiated ambitious economic diversification plans, such as Saudi Arabia's Vision 2030 and the UAE's Vision 2021, to reduce dependence on hydrocarbon revenues and foster sustainable economic growth. These comprehensive plans encompass diversifying into sectors like tourism, finance, real estate, logistics, manufacturing, technology, and renewable energy. By promoting economic diversification, the GCC countries aim to create new job opportunities, boost innovation, enhance competitiveness, and nurture a resilient and diversified economic framework that can withstand fluctuations in global energy markets.

Moreover, the GCC countries' investments in energy infrastructure significantly impact global energy networks. They have developed extensive pipeline systems, providing secure and efficient oil and gas transportation to global markets. Additionally, constructing liquefied natural gas (LNG) terminals and investing in LNG tankers have unlocked new opportunities for the GCC countries to reach distant markets, thereby expanding their global market reach and contributing to the diversification of energy sources for importing countries. These infrastructure developments contribute to expanding global energy networks, enhancing energy security, and facilitating the smooth flow of resources across continents.

The GCC countries also actively engage in international energy organisations such as the Organisation of the Petroleum Exporting Countries (OPEC) and the Gas Exporting Countries Forum (GECF). Through their participation, the GCC countries have successfully influenced global energy policies, fostered collaboration among energy-producing nations and advocated for their collective interests on the international stage. These engagements allow them to effectively address common challenges, including market stability, price volatility, and the shared responsibility of managing global energy resources.

In conclusion, the Gulf Cooperation Council (GCC) is a multifaceted global energy supplier, significantly impacting the world economy. The member countries' abundant reserves, production capacities, energy policies, and participation in international energy organisations collectively shape global energy dynamics. The GCC's strategic investments in energy infrastructure further enhance their role as reliable suppliers, ensuring energy security and stability worldwide. Furthermore, by actively pursuing economic diversification, the GCC countries are taking proactive measures to foster sustainable growth, resilience, and reduced dependence on hydrocarbon revenues in an evolving global energy landscape.

10

HISTORY OF THE GCC AS GLOBAL ENERGY SUPPLIERS

— • —

History of the GCC as Global Energy Suppliers

The Gulf Cooperation Council (GCC) has a rich and complex history as a global energy supplier with a profound impact on the world economy. Since the discovery of vast energy reserves in the region in the mid-20th century, the member countries of the GCC have played a pivotal role in shaping global energy markets. These countries, including Saudi Arabia, Kuwait, Bahrain, Qatar, UAE, and Oman, possess significant oil and gas reserves, making them important contributors to global energy supply and security.

Energy Resources and Production Capacities of GCC Countries

The GCC countries collectively possess some of the world's largest energy reserves, mainly oil and gas. Saudi Arabia, the largest GCC member, sits atop the largest proven oil reserves globally and maintains significant production capacities. The kingdom has invested heavily in upstream exploration and production technologies to maximise recovery rates and improve efficiency. Kuwait possesses abundant oil resources, characterised by high-quality crude oil with low sulphur content, making it highly sought after in global markets. Qatar, known for its vast natural gas reserves, has become a leading liquefied natural gas (LNG) exporter and is considered one of the most reliable suppliers worldwide.

The UAE has substantial crude oil reserves and significant investments in advanced extraction technologies and infrastructure development. It has diversified its energy mix by incorporating renewable energy sources like solar power, aiming to reduce its carbon footprint and enhance sustainability. While possessing smaller oil and gas reserves, Bahrain relies on strategic partnerships and refining capabilities. It has focused on expanding its refining capacity and establishing itself as a regional trading hub, contributing to global energy markets. With its significant oil reserves, Oman has also invested in enhancing recovery techniques to sustain production levels and attract foreign investments.

Energy Supply and Demand Dynamics in the Global Market

The GCC countries closely monitor energy supply and demand dynamics in the global market due to their status as major energy suppliers. They analyse market trends, fluctuations in oil prices, and shifts in global energy demand patterns to ascertain the appropriate adjustments to production levels and export strategies. Continuous monitoring and analysis enable these countries to make informed decisions regarding investments, exploration strategies, and production quotas, aligning their production capacities with market needs and ensuring stable revenues and economic growth.

The GCC countries are crucial in mitigating global energy supply risks, given their large-scale energy exports. They maintain spare production capacities, known as swing capacities, ready to be deployed in case of disruptions in global oil supplies. This strategic approach helps stabilise global energy markets and ensures the availability of resources during emergencies, thereby averting potential crises and reducing price volatility.

Understanding the Impact of GCC Energy Policies on the Global Economy

The energy policies the GCC countries pursue yield substantial implications for the global economy, extending far beyond energy markets alone. As leading energy exporters, any changes in their production levels, export strategies, or pricing mechanisms can significantly influence global energy markets, impacting various sectors and economies worldwide.

The decisions the GCC countries make regarding production quotas have a ripple effect on oil prices and supply dynamics. Their coordinated efforts, often in collaboration with other major oil-producing countries like Russia, have sometimes succeeded in stabilising prices amid market fluctuations. However, fluctuations in oil prices can have both positive and negative implications. While lower prices may benefit oil-importing countries, they pose challenges to the economies heavily reliant on oil exports, necessitating diversification efforts.

The GCC countries have recognised the urgency of diversifying their economies beyond oil and gas. They have initiated ambitious economic diversification plans, such as Saudi Arabia's Vision 2030 and the UAE's Vision 2021, to reduce dependence on hydrocarbon revenues and foster sustainable economic growth. These comprehensive plans encompass diversifying into sectors like tourism, finance, real estate, logistics, manufacturing, technology, and renewable energy. By promoting economic diversification, the GCC countries aim to create new job opportunities, boost innovation, enhance competitiveness, and nurture a resilient and diversified economic framework that can withstand fluctuations in global energy markets.

Moreover, the GCC countries' investments in energy infrastructure significantly impact global energy networks. They have developed extensive pipeline systems, providing secure and efficient oil and gas transportation to global markets. Additionally, constructing liquefied natural gas (LNG) terminals and investing in LNG tankers have unlocked new opportunities for the GCC countries to reach distant markets, thereby expanding their global market reach and contributing to the diversification of energy sources for importing countries. These infrastructure developments contribute to expanding global energy networks, enhancing energy security, and facilitating the smooth flow of resources across continents.

The GCC countries also actively engage in international energy organisations such as the Organisation of the Petroleum Exporting Countries (OPEC) and the Gas Exporting Countries Forum (GECF). Through their participation, the GCC countries have successfully influenced global energy policies, fostered collaboration among energy-producing nations and advocated for their collective interests on the international stage. These engagements allow them to effectively address common challenges, including market stability, price volatility, and the shared responsibility of managing global energy resources.

In conclusion, the Gulf Cooperation Council (GCC) is a multifaceted global energy supplier, significantly impacting the world economy. The member countries' abundant reserves, production capacities, energy policies, and participation in international energy organisations collectively shape global energy dynamics. The GCC's strategic investments in energy infrastructure further enhance their role as reliable suppliers, ensuring energy security and stability worldwide. Furthermore, by actively pursuing economic diversification, the GCC countries are taking proactive measures to foster sustainable growth, resilience, and reduced dependence on hydrocarbon revenues in an evolving global energy landscape.

11

ENERGY RESOURCES AND PRODUCTION CAPACITIES OF GCC COUNTRIES

———— ◆ ————

The Gulf Cooperation Council (GCC) countries, comprising Bahrain, Kuwait, Oman, Qatar, Saudi Arabia, and the United Arab Emirates (UAE), possess significant energy resources that have a pervasive impact on the global energy market. This extensive chapter will delve even deeper into the specifics of these resources and explore the production capacities of each GCC country, shedding light on their profound influence on the global energy landscape.

Saudi Arabia, as the world's largest crude oil exporter, holds approximately 16% of the global proven oil reserves, totalling around 297 billion barrels. The nation's oil production capacity stands at an impressive 12 million barrels per day (bpd), and it actively manages this valuable resource through its state-owned oil company, Saudi Aramco. Saudi Arabia has consistently demonstrated its ability to swiftly increase production to stabilise global markets during periods of supply disruptions or heightened demand. With advanced technologies and extensive infrastructure, the country efficiently extracts, refines, and exports substantial volumes of oil to meet both domestic consumption and international demand.

Qatar, another noteworthy player in the GCC, ranks as the third-largest holder of natural gas reserves worldwide, with approximately 890 trillion cubic feet. While Qatar is also an exporter of oil, it has emerged as a leading producer and exporter of liquefied natural gas (LNG). Leveraging its cutting-edge LNG production facilities, Qatar has become a prominent player in meeting the growing global demand for clean and versatile natural gas. Its LNG exports have propelled Qatar to be one of the top global suppliers, significantly contributing to its economic growth. The country's LNG projects, such as the North Field expansion, aim to further bolster its production capabilities in the coming years.

Kuwait, a significant oil producer within the GCC, possesses about 6% of global reserves, with around 101 billion barrels. The country benefits from advanced infrastructure for oil extraction, refining, and exportation. The state-owned Kuwait Petroleum Corporation (KPC) oversees the nation's resources, ensuring a stable flow of petroleum products worldwide. Kuwait's refining capacity, combined with its strategic investments in downstream operations, supports its goal of diversifying its energy sector and expanding its downstream petrochemical industry. The Al-Zour Refinery, currently under construction, will further enhance Kuwait's refining capabilities upon completion.

The UAE, while not possessing the same vast oil reserves as Saudi Arabia or Kuwait, has been incessantly investing in the development of its oil and gas production capacities. The country's current reserves stand at around 97 billion barrels, but it has substantially augmented its production capacities through technological advancements and innovative projects. The UAE is committed to maximising the value from its oil resources, including the development of sour gas fields such as the Shah Gas Field, which contributes to its overall natural gas production. Additionally, the UAE has made considerable investments in downstream industries, including refining and petrochemicals, further enhancing its role as a vital player in the global energy market. The UAE's energy diversification strategy promotes investments in renewable energy sources, with notable projects like the Mohammed bin Rashid Al Maktoum Solar Park and the Barakah Nuclear Power Plant.

Oman, although considered smaller in terms of reserves compared to its neighbouring GCC countries, has focused on expanding its hydrocarbon resources and production capacities. Its current oil reserves amount to approximately 4.9 billion barrels, and the government actively pursues exploration and development to increase this figure. Oman's commitment to expanding its energy sector includes the development of both onshore and offshore oil and gas fields, supporting its economy and future energy security. The Duqm Refinery and Petrochemical Complex, a joint venture between Oman Oil Company and Kuwait Petroleum International, is set to enhance Oman's refining capabilities upon its completion.

The energy resources of the GCC countries have an immeasurable impact on the global energy market. These nations not only have the ability to influence global oil prices but also play a crucial role in ensuring stable oil supplies, particularly during times of supply disruptions or geopolitical uncertainties. Their collective efforts contribute to maintaining a balanced and secure energy market worldwide.

Furthermore, the GCC countries have embraced a vision for a sustainable future by promoting renewable energy sources. With abundant solar and wind resources, the region has launched numerous initiatives and projects to harness clean and sustainable energy. Saudi Arabia, for instance, aims to develop 58.7 GW of renewable energy capacity by 2030, making it one of the largest solar markets globally. The UAE has embarked on similar ventures, such as the ambitious Masdar City project and the establishment of the Abu Dhabi Renewable Energy Corporation, showcasing its commitment to sustainable development. Qatar, too, has made strides in renewable energy, with initiatives like the Qatar National Vision 2030 guiding its sustainable energy ambitions.

In conclusion, the GCC countries possess extensive and diverse energy resources that greatly influence the global energy landscape. From Saudi Arabia's colossal oil reserves and production capacities to Qatar's leading role in the LNG sector, and the systematic developments in Kuwait, the UAE, and Oman, these nations shape the energy market's dynamics. Moreover, their growing investments in renewable energy sources demonstrate a collective commitment to a sustainable and diversified energy future, ensuring long-term energy security while mitigating the environmental impact of energy production and consumption.

12

ENERGY SUPPLY AND DEMAND DYNAMICS IN THE GLOBAL MARKET

— • —

E nergy supply and demand dynamics play a crucial role in shaping the global market. As population growth continues to surge, the need for energy to power industries, infrastructure, and everyday activities intensifies. Understanding the intricate trends and shifts in energy supply and demand becomes essential to assessing the formidable challenges and enticing opportunities in the global energy landscape.

One of the key factors significantly impacting energy supply and demand dynamics is the availability and accessibility of energy resources. For decades, traditional fossil fuels like coal, oil, and natural gas have held dominance as primary energy sources. However, the escalating focus on sustainable and clean energy alternatives has gradually diversified energy sources.

Renewable energy options, including solar, wind, hydroelectric, and geothermal power, have gained significant traction as countries strive to reduce their carbon emissions and transition to a greener and more sustainable future. The development and deployment of renewable energy technologies have created new avenues for energy supply. Solar power, for example, has seen remarkable growth, with photovoltaic installations increasing exponentially over the past decade. Wind power has also experienced rapid expansion, with offshore wind farms becoming increasingly common in coastal areas. Despite their intermittent nature and dependency on weather conditions, advancements in energy storage technologies are helping to mitigate the challenges related to the reliability and availability of renewable energy.

Geographical distribution plays another vital role in shaping energy supply and demand dynamics. Certain countries, such as the Gulf Cooperation Council (GCC) member states, are abundantly blessed with fossil fuel reserves, which possess significant quantities of oil and gas. These countries have historically played a central role in global energy markets, as their resources are vital for meeting the immense global energy demand.

The Gulf region's abundant oil reserves have allowed it to become a major global exporter and a key player in the energy market. However, the region's dependence on a single resource exposes it to potential vulnerabilities, such as price fluctuations caused by global supply and demand imbalances or geopolitical tensions. Therefore, in recent years, the GCC countries have proactively worked to diversify their economies and reduce their reliance on oil revenue, aiming for long-term sustainability. They invest in renewable energy projects, such as solar and wind farms, and explore opportunities in other industries, including tourism, finance, and technology.

On the other hand, countries lacking sufficient domestic energy resources heavily rely on energy imports to meet their demand. The countries within the BRICS+ group, with their growing populations and industrialisation, face the perpetual challenge of balancing energy supply and demand. They often rely on energy imports to bridge the gap and strive to diversify their energy sources to enhance their energy security.

As the largest member of the BRICS+ group, China has experienced rapid economic growth and soaring energy demand over the past few decades. Traditionally, the country has heavily relied on coal for energy, resulting in significant environmental and public health challenges. However, recognising these issues, China has been actively transitioning towards cleaner energy sources, including renewable energy and natural gas. The country leads the world in renewable energy investments and is a major player in the solar and wind power sectors. Its commitment to reducing carbon emissions and transitioning to a low-carbon economy has led to a significant increase in deploying renewable energy technologies.

India, another prominent member of the BRICS+ consortium, is also witnessing a tremendous increase in energy demand. With a population of over 1.3 billion people and ongoing industrialisation, India faces multiple challenges in meeting its energy needs while mitigating environmental impacts. The country has set ambitious renewable energy targets and actively promotes investments in solar, wind, and hydroelectric power projects. India is also pushing for greater energy efficiency measures and exploring ways to improve its infrastructure to ensure a reliable and sustainable energy supply.

Geopolitical factors further influence the interplay between energy supply and demand. The concentration of energy resources in certain regions creates dependencies and vulnerabilities, posing risks to energy security. Political tensions, conflicts, and disruptions in energy-producing regions can have far-reaching consequences on global energy markets, leading to supply shortages and price fluctuations.

Recent geopolitical developments, such as trade disputes and sanctions, have underscored the importance of diversifying energy sources and supply routes to reduce vulnerabilities. Countries are exploring energy partnerships and collaborations to enhance their energy security. Initiatives like the Belt and Road Initiative (BRI), led by China, aim to strengthen energy connectivity across regions, promoting energy trade and interdependence.

Moreover, the global transition towards sustainable energy and efforts to reduce carbon emissions reshape energy demand patterns. As governments, businesses, and consumers prioritise clean energy alternatives, the demand for fossil fuels is expected to decline. This monumental shift towards renewable energy sources and energy-efficient technologies presents both challenges and opportunities for energy-producing countries, particularly those heavily reliant on fossil fuel exports.

Understanding the intricate dynamics of energy supply and demand in the global market is critical for policymakers, businesses, and stakeholders. It enables the identification of potential vulnerabilities, anticipation of market trends, and development of comprehensive energy security and sustainability strategies. Increasing cooperation and collaboration between countries, such as the BRICS+ consortium and the Gulf Cooperation Council, become increasingly important in addressing these challenges collectively and fostering a more resilient and sustainable energy future.

In the subsequent chapters, we will delve deeper into the energy dynamics between the BRICS+ countries and the Gulf Cooperation Council, extensively exploring their respective energy resources, dependencies, and collaborations. By meticulously analysing the supply and demand dynamics in the global energy market, we aim to provide profound insights into the evolving energy landscape and its profound implications for global sustainability and economic development.

13

THE IMPACT OF GCC ENERGY POLICIES ON THE GLOBAL ECONOMY

— • —

The Gulf Cooperation Council (GCC) countries, primarily known for their abundant oil and gas reserves, play a significant role in shaping the global energy landscape. Their energy policies have far-reaching implications for the global economy, influencing energy prices, supply and demand dynamics, geopolitical relationships, and sustainable development.

1. Energy Prices: The GCC countries are major oil exporters, and their energy policies directly impact global oil prices. The GCC has become known as a swing producer, adjusting its oil production levels to stabilise the global market. By increasing or decreasing production, the GCC can influence oil prices, affecting the profitability of oil-producing nations worldwide. Fluctuations in oil prices have implications for energy-intensive industries, transportation costs, and consumer spending patterns.

The GCC's ability to regulate oil prices has been evident in its response to global energy crises. During the 1973 oil embargo, when the Organisation of Arab Petroleum Exporting Countries (OAPEC) imposed an oil embargo on countries supporting Israel, the GCC member countries significantly raised oil prices, resulting in supply disruptions. This event caused a global economic downturn marked by soaring inflation rates and slow economic growth in oil-importing countries. Similarly, during the 2014-2016 oil price collapse, the GCC maintained high production levels to protect market share, leading to a significant decline in oil prices. While this hurt oil-exporting countries, it relieved oil-importing nations and stimulated economic activity in various sectors.

2. Energy Security: The GCC's energy policies also contribute to global security. As a major supplier, the GCC ensures a stable flow of oil and gas to global markets, helping to

safeguard energy supplies for countries heavily dependent on fossil fuels. Any disruptions or instability in the GCC's energy production and distribution could severely affect the global energy market, leading to price spikes and economic uncertainties.

To enhance energy security, the GCC has invested in infrastructure projects, such as pipelines, terminals, and export facilities, to improve the efficiency and reliability of energy transportation. These developments have strengthened the GCC's position as a key energy exporter and diversified transportation routes, reducing the vulnerability of global energy supply chains to geopolitical tensions and maritime chokepoints.

Moreover, the GCC has recognised the importance of diversifying its own energy sources to ensure long-term energy security. In recent years, several GCC countries, including Saudi Arabia and the United Arab Emirates, have significantly invested in renewable energy projects. The advancement of solar and wind power technologies in the region has the potential to complement traditional oil and gas resources, reduce carbon emissions, and address climate change challenges. These renewable energy initiatives contribute to the GCC's energy diversification goals and promote sustainable development at a global level.

3. Economic Interdependencies: The GCC's energy policies have fostered economic interdependencies with other countries. The GCC has forged strategic partnerships with energy-consuming and energy-producing nations through long-term supply contracts and investments in energy infrastructure. These economic interdependencies create mutually beneficial relationships and contribute to economic growth and stability and technological advancements in the energy sector.

For energy-consuming nations, such as the United States, Europe, and Asia, the GCC's reliable oil and gas supplies support their economic activities, ensuring a steady energy supply for industrial production, transportation, and electricity generation. In return, the GCC benefits from these partnerships through technology transfers, knowledge sharing, and investment inflows that can help diversify their economies and reduce their reliance on fossil fuels.

Furthermore, the GCC's investment in renewable energy projects has opened up new avenues for collaboration and economic growth. Efforts to promote clean energy technologies have attracted international firms and expertise, facilitating the transfer of knowledge and fostering innovation in the GCC countries. These advancements contribute to local economic development and benefit the global renewable energy industry, promoting its expansion and adoption in other regions.

4. Technological Advancements: As the GCC explores technological advancements in the energy sector, including advanced drilling techniques, enhanced oil recovery methods, and digitalisation, it not only enhances its own production capabilities but also contributes to the global energy supply. Adopting cleaner energy technologies, such as carbon capture and storage, smart grid systems, and energy efficiency measures, can have positive environmental implications, reducing greenhouse gas emissions and addressing global climate change concerns.

The GCC countries have heavily invested in research and development to unlock unconventional and offshore oil and gas resources. Advances in seismic imaging, drilling technologies, and reservoir management techniques have enabled the extraction of previously inaccessible hydrocarbon reserves, expanding global energy reserves and enhancing energy security.

Similarly, the GCC's push towards renewable energy sources has accelerated the deployment of innovative technologies and brought down the costs of solar and wind power generation. These advancements have made renewable energy more economically viable and contributed to the global energy transition. The GCC's commitment to technological advancements in energy benefits its own energy industry and contributes to global energy innovation and sustainability.

5. Geopolitical Relationships: The GCC's energy policies are closely intertwined with geopolitical relationships, particularly with major energy consumers like the United States, Europe, and Asia. Energy trade and cooperation shape diplomatic ties and influence security arrangements among nations. The GCC's role as a reliable energy supplier enables it to leverage its energy resources to enhance its geopolitical influence and establish strategic alliances.

In recent years, the GCC has sought to expand its energy markets beyond traditional buyers, looking towards emerging Asian economies like China and India. This shift aligns with the growing energy demands of these nations and allows the GCC to diversify its customer base, reducing its reliance on a few significant markets.

Furthermore, the GCC's energy policies can also impact regional geopolitics. Energy-intensive industries and diverse natural resources can shape geopolitical rivalries and alliances within the GCC region itself. As the competition for energy resources and markets intensifies, it creates a complex geopolitical landscape, influencing regional stability and shaping international relations. Understanding the intricate connections between energy policies, geopolitics, and economic interests is crucial for effectively navigating the evolving dynamics of the global energy landscape.

In conclusion, the GCC's energy policies profoundly impact the global economy. As a major source of oil and gas, the GCC's decisions regarding production levels, diversification efforts, technological advancements, and geopolitical relationships have far-reaching implications. Recognising the multi-dimensional effects of GCC energy policies is essential for policymakers, businesses, and energy consumers worldwide as they strive to adapt to the challenges and opportunities presented by the energy transition and sustainable development goals.

14

BRICS+ AND GULF COOPERATION COUNCIL: INTERSECTING INTERESTS

— • —

A Comparative Analysis of BRICS+ and GCC Alliances

The BRICS+ consortium, comprising Brazil, Russia, India, China, South Africa, and additional partner countries, and the Gulf Cooperation Council (GCC), consisting of Saudi Arabia, the United Arab Emirates, Qatar, Kuwait, Bahrain, and Oman, are two major economic and geopolitical entities with intersecting interests. While BRICS+ is a forum for emerging economies seeking to promote economic cooperation and enhance their global influence, the GCC is a regional organisation focused on regional stability and economic integration within the Gulf region.

Complementarities and Potential Collaborations Between BRICS+ and Gulf Countries

Despite their distinct characteristics, there are several areas where BRICS+ and Gulf countries can find complementarities and potential collaborations.

Energy Cooperation:

One area that stands out is energy. The Gulf countries possess vast reserves of oil and gas, making them significant players in the global energy market. Meanwhile, BRICS+ economies have a high demand for energy resources to fuel their rapid economic growth. This provides opportunities for energy cooperation, investment, and technology transfer between the two groups. Gulf countries can benefit from the demand for their energy resources from BRICS+ countries, which can help diversify their economies and reduce reliance on a single market. At the same time, BRICS+ countries can ensure a steady energy supply by collaborating with Gulf countries to secure affordable and stable energy sources. Joint ventures in the energy sector, exploration and production partnerships, and investments in renewable energy projects are some ways in which BRICS+ and Gulf countries can enhance cooperation and create a mutually beneficial energy landscape.

Trade and Investment:

Another area of potential collaboration is trade and investment. The large and rapidly growing consumer markets in BRICS+ countries offer attractive opportunities for Gulf countries to expand their export base, diversify their economies, and attract foreign direct investment. The increasing middle-class populations in BRICS+ countries have created a new wave of consumers with changing demands, presenting immense potential for Gulf countries to export their goods, services, and expertise. Furthermore, with their strategic geographic location, Gulf countries can serve as logistics hubs and gateways for BRICS+ countries to enter the Gulf region and access other global markets. By exploring avenues for greater trade facilitation, investment protection, and economic integration, both BRICS+ and Gulf countries can create a win-win situation by leveraging their respective strengths. Bilateral and multilateral trade agreements, investment promotion and protection frameworks, and the establishment of joint economic zones can greatly enhance economic ties between the two groups.

Opportunities for Economic and Technological Partnerships

BRICS+ countries have been making significant strides in innovation and technology. Collaborative efforts between BRICS+ and Gulf countries in research and development, technology transfer, and joint ventures can lead to mutually beneficial outcomes.

Research and Development:

Gulf countries can benefit from technological advancements achieved by BRICS+ countries, particularly in sectors such as renewable energy, artificial intelligence, biotechnology, and healthcare. Collaborating in research and development projects can help Gulf countries overcome technological gaps and enhance their own capabilities. Similarly, Gulf countries can share their expertise in the areas of hydrocarbon exploration, extraction technologies, and petrochemical industries, which remain crucial to the development of BRICS+ economies. By pooling resources, sharing knowledge, and jointly investing in R&D initiatives, both BRICS+ and Gulf countries can accelerate innovation, address common challenges, and foster sustainable development.

Technology Transfer:

Through technology transfer, BRICS+ countries can access advanced technologies developed by Gulf countries, enabling them to boost their own industrial capabilities and contribute to economic growth. Additionally, joint ventures and partnerships between BRICS+ and Gulf companies can facilitate the transfer of knowledge, expertise, and technology in various sectors, ranging from infrastructure development to telecommunications and manufacturing. Establishing technology incubators, innovation centres, and technology parks can provide a platform for collaboration and ensure a steady exchange of technological advancements between the two groups.

Mutual Challenges and Ways to Overcome Them

While BRICS+ and Gulf countries share common interests, some challenges must be addressed.

Economic Diversification:

One of the primary challenges both BRICS+ and Gulf countries face is the diversification of their economies. Both groups know the need to reduce their reliance on fossil fuels and develop more sustainable and diversified economies. Cooperation between BRICS+ and Gulf countries in sharing experiences, best practices, and investments in renewable energy, technology infrastructure, and other sectors can help overcome this challenge. Gulf countries can learn from the experiences of BRICS+ countries in their transition towards greener economies, while BRICS+ countries can benefit from the expertise of Gulf countries in developing sustainable infrastructure and managing energy resources. Moreover, both groups can collaborate on initiatives that promote entrepreneurship, innovation, and small and medium-sized enterprises (SMEs) to drive economic diversification.

Geo-political Tensions:

Another challenge is geopolitical tensions and conflicts in certain regions. The BRICS+ consortium and the GCC must actively engage in diplomatic efforts to address conflicts and promote regional stability. Confidence-building measures, dialogue, and mediation can reduce tensions and foster cooperation. Both groups can utilise their diplomatic channels, existing platforms, and peace initiatives to mitigate conflicts, encourage dialogue, and promote peaceful resolutions. Ensuring that regional stability is not compromised is essential for facilitating the development of conducive environments for collaboration and fostering trust among member states.

Conclusion:

In conclusion, the BRICS+ consortium and the Gulf Cooperation Council have intersecting interests in various areas such as energy, trade, investment, and technology. By leveraging their respective strengths and addressing common challenges, BRICS+ and Gulf countries can enhance collaboration and contribute to regional and global development. The opportunities for energy cooperation, trade and investment partnerships, economic diversification, and technological collaborations present immense potential for mutual growth and prosperity. Both BRICS+ and Gulf countries must foster dialogue, build trust, and forge stronger ties to capitalise on these opportunities and create a sustainable and prosperous future. By deepening their collaboration, embracing economic integration, and promoting technological advancements, BRICS+ and Gulf countries can collectively shape the future global order and establish a more balanced and diversified global economy.

15

A COMPARATIVE ANALYSIS OF BRICS+ AND GCC ALLIANCES

— ⚬ —

T he BRICS+ consortium and the Gulf Cooperation Council (GCC) are two significant alliances that hold strategic importance in the global order. While the
BRICS+ consists of emerging economies such as Brazil, Russia, India, China, and South
Africa, the GCC comprises six Gulf countries, namely Saudi Arabia, United Arab Emirates, Bahrain, Oman, Qatar, and Kuwait. A comparative analysis of these alliances provides a comprehensive understanding of their similarities, differences, and potential for
collaboration.

Both the BRICS+ and GCC alliances share common characteristics that contribute
to their significance in the global arena. Firstly, they are regional alliances formed by
countries with shared interests and long-term objectives. The BRICS+ was established
to enhance cooperation among its member states and promote economic growth and
development. This alliance serves as a platform for these emerging economies to engage
in dialogue, address common challenges, and collaborate on various issues of mutual
concern. In contrast, the GCC was formed to foster economic, political, and security
cooperation among the Gulf countries. Initially established as a response to regional
challenges, the GCC has evolved into a platform for its member states to strengthen their
unity, promote stability, and advance their common interests.

Secondly, both BRICS+ and the GCC alliances significantly impact the global economy. The BRICS+ countries collectively make up a substantial proportion of global GDP
and trade, leading to their growing importance in shaping global economic policies. China, in particular, has emerged as a global economic powerhouse, surpassing many Western
powers in terms of GDP and trade volume. Its industrial and manufacturing capabilities,
as well as its massive consumer market, have positioned it as a key player in the global

economy. With its large population and the potential for significant economic growth, India is also contributing significantly to the expansion and influence of the BRICS+. Additionally, Russia's vast natural resources, advanced technological capabilities, and Brazil and South Africa's regional leadership roles and emerging economic potential play essential roles in the collective strength of the alliance.

Similarly, the GCC countries possess vast energy reserves, particularly oil and gas, which are important in the global energy market. The GCC countries exert significant influence over energy security and prices worldwide through their collective influence. As the largest oil exporter among the GCC countries, Saudi Arabia is often regarded as the key player in shaping global oil policies, and its decisions can significantly impact the global economy. The United Arab Emirates, Qatar, and Kuwait are also major oil and gas producers with significant reserves, and they utilise their energy resources to assert their influence regionally and beyond. Their collective capabilities make the GCC a critical player in the energy realm, enabling it to contribute significantly to global energy stability and supply.

Despite these similarities, there are notable differences between the two alliances. One significant difference lies in their levels of development and economic structures. The BRICS+ consortium represents a more diverse set of economies than the GCC. While China and India have experienced rapid economic growth, becoming among the largest economies in the world, their developmental challenges and structural issues still persist. However, their potential to contribute to the global economy and influence regional affairs cannot be overlooked. With its extensive reserves of natural resources and advanced technological sectors, Russia has emerged from a turbulent transition period and asserted itself as a significant global player. Brazil and South Africa, while facing their own unique economic challenges, have made considerable progress in establishing themselves as regional leaders and emerging economies with substantial growth potential. In comparison, the GCC consists of smaller, oil-dependent countries with relatively homogeneous economies. Their developmental challenges lie more in diversifying their economies and reducing their dependence on oil revenues. However, their collective wealth and strategic location have enabled them to secure robust economic growth and development.

Geopolitically, the BRICS+ alliance seeks to challenge the dominance of Western powers and create a fairer global economic system. Its members advocate for a more balanced representation in global governance institutions, such as the International Monetary Fund (IMF) and the World Bank, and call for reforms to reflect the current geopolitical realities better. The BRICS+ countries strive to foster multi-polarity in global decision-making and promote more inclusive international trade practices. In contrast, the GCC primarily focuses on regional security and stability. Situated in a volatile region, the GCC alliance seeks to protect its members' interests, maintain a balance of power in the Gulf, and safeguard against external threats. The GCC countries often engage in defence and security cooperation to counter common challenges, such as terrorism and regional conflicts, ensuring the stability of vital energy shipping routes.

Despite these differences, there is significant potential for collaboration between the BRICS+ and GCC alliances. Both alliances possess complementary strengths that can be leveraged for mutual benefits. For example, the BRICS+ countries can benefit from the GCC's energy resources, ensuring a stable and diverse energy supply for their rapidly growing economies. Additionally, the GCC can benefit from the BRICS+'s technological advancements and investment opportunities, contributing to their ongoing economic diversification efforts. By engaging in technology transfer and knowledge sharing, the BRICS+ alliance can assist the GCC countries in developing new sectors and enhancing their economic competitiveness.

Collaboration between BRICS+ and the GCC can extend beyond economic cooperation. Given their geopolitical influence and regional significance, these alliances can work together to address common challenges, such as terrorism, regional conflicts, and climate change. By leveraging their collective resources and capabilities, BRICS+ and the GCC can play a more significant role in shaping global security agendas, promoting sustainable development, and contributing to conflict resolution efforts. Cooperation between the BRICS+ alliance and the GCC could lead to joint initiatives in technology transfer, knowledge sharing, and capacity-building programmes. These collaborations would mutually benefit the member states, foster closer relationships, and contribute to economic growth and development in both regions.

In conclusion, a comprehensive comparative analysis of BRICS+ and GCC alliances highlights their similarities, differences, and potential for collaboration. While they differ regarding economic structures, geopolitical priorities, and global influence, these alliances possess unique strengths that can be harnessed to address common challenges and reshape the global order. Recognising the potential synergies between these alliances and developing deeper collaborations and partnerships is essential for policymakers and decision-makers in the international arena. By working together, BRICS+ and the GCC can forge stronger alliances, amplify their impact, and contribute to a more balanced and sustainable global order.

16

COMPLEMENTARITIES AND POTENTIAL COLLABORATIONS BETWEEN BRICS+ AND GULF COUNTRIES

— • —

The relationship between the BRICS+ consortium and the Gulf Cooperation Council (GCC) presents significant opportunities for complementarities and potential collaborations across various dimensions. Both entities possess unique strengths and resources that, when combined, can lead to mutually beneficial outcomes and contribute to global economic growth, technological advancements, cultural exchange, and regional security.

Economically, the BRICS+ countries—Brazil, Russia, India, China, South Africa, and the newly added countries—offer immense potential as emerging markets with expanding consumer bases and diverse manufacturing capabilities. These countries provide attractive investment opportunities for the Gulf countries, which possess substantial financial resources and expertise in sectors such as energy, real estate, and infrastructure development. The GCC's investments in BRICS+ countries diversify their portfolios and support the growth and development of BRICS+ economies, thereby creating a win-win situation for both sides.

Furthermore, the strategic geographical locations of both BRICS+ and Gulf countries play a crucial role in their complementarity. Gulf countries situated at the crossroads of Europe, Africa, and Asia serve as important trade hubs, connecting these regions and facilitating the movement of goods and services. This position can be leveraged to enhance collaboration between BRICS+ and the Gulf countries, as both regions can benefit from improved connectivity, reduced trade barriers, and efficient logistics networks. Exploring the potential for joint infrastructure projects, such as ports, railways, and highways, can enhance interregional trade and bolster economic ties.

In addition to trade and investment, energy cooperation is a significant area of synergy between BRICS+ and the Gulf countries. The GCC countries are globally recognised as major oil and gas exporters, accounting for a substantial share of the world's hydrocarbon production. Collaborating with BRICS+ countries, which have growing energy demands driven by rapid urbanisation and industrialisation, can ensure both regions' stable and secure energy supply. Energy partnerships can involve exploration and production projects, renewable energy investments, research and development in clean technologies, and knowledge exchange to promote energy efficiency and sustainability.

Technological collaborations present another compelling avenue for cooperation. BRICS+ countries have made remarkable progress in sectors such as information technology, biotechnology, renewable energy, and space exploration. Partnering with the GCC countries, which aspire to transition to knowledge-based economies, can facilitate knowledge transfer, technology sharing, and joint research projects. Establishing technology parks, innovation clusters, and entrepreneurship initiatives can further foster creativity and sustainable development in both regions. Collaborative efforts can also leverage artificial intelligence, robotics, big data, and internet-of-things technologies to drive digital transformation and enhance productivity across various sectors.

Cultural and people-to-people exchanges are vital to building strong bilateral relationships and fostering mutual understanding. Cultural diplomacy initiatives, such as art exhibitions, film festivals, music collaborations, and literary exchanges, can showcase the rich heritage and diversity of BRICS+ and Gulf countries. These initiatives promote cultural understanding and support the tourism industry as travellers seek to explore these regions' unique traditions, history, and natural beauty. By encouraging more tourism flows and facilitating visa processes, both BRICS+ and the Gulf countries can unlock economic benefits and create lasting impressions in the minds of visitors.

Collaboration between BRICS+ and the Gulf countries is not limited to economic, technological, and cultural dimensions; it extends to addressing common global challenges. Cooperation in areas such as climate change mitigation, sustainable development, cybersecurity, healthcare, counterterrorism, and regional security can strengthen the collective response of both entities. Sharing experiences, expertise, and best practices can lead to innovative solutions, improved governance frameworks, and enhanced security initiatives. Collaborative efforts in these areas will benefit BRICS+ and the Gulf countries and contribute to global stability, peace, and prosperity.

Moreover, it is essential to recognise the potential of joint research and innovation platforms to drive scientific advancements and address global challenges. BRICS+ and the Gulf countries can establish cooperative frameworks that promote academic collaborations, knowledge sharing, and technology transfer in areas such as health research, climate science, biotechnology, and sustainable agriculture. By pooling resources and expertise, both sides can accelerate progress towards the United Nations Sustainable Development Goals and find innovative solutions to the world's most pressing issues.

In conclusion, the complementarities and potential collaborations between BRICS+ and the Gulf countries offer various economic, technological, cultural, and security opportunities. Both entities can shape a more integrated and prosperous future by leveraging their shared strengths and resources. Governments, businesses, educational institutions, and civil society organisations must actively explore and capitalise on these opportunities to foster fruitful partnerships and achieve sustainable development. These collaborations are essential for the participating countries and can positively impact the global order by promoting inclusive growth, innovation, cultural diversity, and regional stability.

17

OPPORTUNITIES FOR ECONOMIC AND TECHNOLOGICAL PARTNERSHIPS

— ◆ —

I n this chapter, we explore the potential economic and technological partnerships between the BRICS+ consortium and the Gulf Cooperation Council (GCC) countries. Both entities possess significant economic resources, diverse industries, and emerging technological capabilities, which create a favourable environment for collaboration and mutual benefit. By focusing on areas such as trade and investment, infrastructure development, diversification of industries, innovation and research, start-up ecosystems, and digital connectivity, we aim to identify more opportunities to strengthen these partnerships.

1. Trade and Investment Opportunities

a) Market Potential: The BRICS+ countries, encompassing Brazil, Russia, India, China, and South Africa, along with the GCC nations of Saudi Arabia, the United Arab Emirates, Qatar, Kuwait, Bahrain, and Oman, boast extensive consumer markets. Leveraging this potential through increased trade and investment can create economic growth and provide new business opportunities in both regions.

b) Barriers Reduction: Exploring avenues to reduce trade barriers, such as tariffs and non-tariff barriers, can boost trade volumes and improve market access. Bilateral and multilateral agreements can streamline business procedures, facilitate trade flows, and encourage investment.

c) Sector-Specific Collaboration: Identifying sector-specific collaboration opportunities can enhance economic ties. For instance, the BRICS+ countries excel in sectors like information technology, manufacturing, and agriculture, while the GCC nations have strengths in industries such as petrochemicals, tourism, and financial services. Joint ventures and knowledge-sharing in these sectors can result in diversified revenue streams and economic resilience.

2. Infrastructure Development

a) Financing Mechanisms: Collaborative efforts to finance major infrastructure projects can drive economic growth and improve regional connectivity. Establishing dedicated mechanisms, such as investment funds, project financing platforms, and public-private partnerships, can attract capital and efficiently allocate resources.

b) Sustainable Infrastructure: Focusing on sustainable infrastructure development ensures long-term economic benefits while addressing environmental challenges. Integrating renewable energy, green building practises, and efficient transport systems can contribute to climate change mitigation and the fulfilment of the United Nations Sustainable Development Goals.

c) Connectivity Enhancement: Strengthening connectivity between the BRICS+ consortium and the GCC countries through infrastructure projects, such as ports, roads, railways, and digital networks, can enhance trade and people-to-people exchanges. Coordinated efforts to improve logistics networks, streamline customs procedures, and harmonise standards can facilitate smoother transportation of goods and services.

3. Diversification of Industries

a) Technology and Knowledge Transfer: Collaborative ventures in technology and knowledge transfer can supercharge economies and boost innovation. The BRICS+ consortium's advanced technological capabilities, including artificial intelligence, robotics, and biotechnology, can be shared with the GCC countries, enabling them to leapfrog into cutting-edge industries.

b) Human Capital Development: Fostering human capital development is essential for economic diversification. Promoting entrepreneurship, vocational training programmes, and partnerships between educational institutions can equip the workforce with the required skills, facilitating industry transformation.

c) Strategic Sector Focus: Identifying strategic sectors that align with the economic visions of both parties can drive targeted collaborations. For instance, collaboration in the aerospace and defence industry aligns with Russia's expertise in these sectors and the GCC countries' aspirations for aerospace development. Similarly, partnerships in sustainable agriculture can leverage Brazil's agricultural innovations and address the GCC nations' food security concerns.

4. Innovation and Research

a) Joint Research Initiatives: Facilitating joint research initiatives between academia, research institutions, and industry can enhance knowledge exchange, foster innovation, and address common challenges. Specialised research clusters, funding programmes, and dedicated platforms for collaboration can promote breakthroughs in areas like healthcare, biotechnology, and renewable energy.

b) Technology Parks and Incubators: Establishing technology parks and incubators that encourage cross-border collaboration can facilitate the growth of innovative start-ups and amplify technological advancements. These platforms can provide access to funding, mentorship, and shared resources, nurturing a vibrant ecosystem conducive to entrepreneurship.

c) Intellectual Property Protection: Robust intellectual property protection frameworks and enforcement mechanisms foster innovation and research collaborations. Establishing transparent and reliable systems for registering patents, trademarks, and copyrights enhances confidence among innovators and incentivises knowledge-sharing.

5. Start-up Ecosystems

a) Cross-Continental Incubators: Creating cross-continental incubators tailored to the specific needs of start-ups can facilitate knowledge exchange, mentorship, and access to a broader market. These incubators can foster cultural exchange, promote joint innovation, and provide a platform for start-ups from both regions to expand their network.

b) Investment Networks: Establishing investment networks, venture capital funds, and angel investor communities spanning the BRICS+ consortium and the GCC countries can unlock start-up funding opportunities. Encouraging angel investments, matching funds by governments, and investor roadshows can boost entrepreneurial activity and attract investments into promising ventures.

c) Skilled Labour Mobility: Promoting skilled labour mobility through streamlined visa processes and mutual recognition of qualifications can facilitate knowledge transfer and talent exchange. This mobility enables start-ups to access a diverse talent pool and build multinational teams, fostering innovation and promoting cultural integration.

6. Digital Connectivity

a) Cybersecurity Cooperation: Enhancing cybersecurity cooperation between the BRICS+ consortium and the GCC countries is vital, given the growing digital landscape. Collaborative efforts to share best practices, establish information-sharing frameworks, and develop joint cybersecurity solutions can protect digital infrastructure and safeguard against cyber threats.

b) E-commerce Platforms: Encouraging the development and integration of e-commerce platforms can enhance cross-border trade, facilitate secure online transactions, and expand market access for small and medium-sized enterprises (SMEs). Joint marketing campaigns and cross-border digital payment systems can bridge the gap between buyers and sellers.

c) Digital Skills Development: Investing in digital skills development and promoting digital literacy programmes enable inclusive growth and bridge the digital divide. Emphasising coding, data analytics, and digital marketing skills equip individuals with the necessary tools to participate actively in the digital economy.

Conclusion:

The potential for economic and technological partnerships between the BRICS+ consortium and the Gulf Cooperation Council countries is vast. By leveraging market potential, collaborating on infrastructure development, diversifying industries, fostering innovation and research, nurturing start-up ecosystems, and promoting digital connectivity, the two entities can lay a foundation for sustained economic growth and mutual benefits. Building a favourable business environment, including streamlined regulations, transparent legal frameworks, and efficient dispute resolution mechanisms, is key to attracting investment and fostering long-term collaborations. By embracing these opportunities, the BRICS+ consortium and the GCC can further strengthen their ties, contributing to global economic growth, technological advancement, and shared prosperity.

18

MUTUAL CHALLENGES AND WAYS TO OVERCOME THEM

— • —

In this chapter, we will examine the various challenges that are faced by the BRICS+ consortium and the Gulf Cooperation Council (GCC) in their pursuit of their respective goals. These challenges are multifaceted and include economic disparities, political systems, security threats, climate change, environmental concerns, technological advancements, and cultural and linguistic barriers. By exploring these areas in depth, we can gain a better understanding of the complexities involved in overcoming these challenges. We also propose comprehensive strategies and collaborative approaches to help address these issues.

1. Economic Disparities:

Economic disparities among member countries pose a significant challenge for both BRICS+ and the GCC. While some members have robust economies, others struggle with development and stability. To address this issue, cooperation platforms should prioritise inclusive growth strategies. This can be done through capacity-building programmes, knowledge sharing on best practices, and promoting trade and investment among member nations. Technical assistance programmes can foster economic diversification, entrepreneurship, and innovation in economically weaker members, thereby reducing the consortium's overall economic disparities.

2. Diverse Political Systems:

The diverse political systems within BRICS+ and the GCC present challenges in finding common ground and ensuring effective decision-making. To tackle this hurdle, respecting each other's sovereignty and promoting democratic principles are essential. Regular political consultations, exchanges of governance models, and creating platforms for dialogue can facilitate mutual understanding and trust among member nations. Such engagements can foster a better comprehension of each other's political systems and enable finding commonalities for effective collaboration.

3. Security Threats:

Both BRICS+ and the GCC face common security challenges, including terrorism, regional conflicts, and non-state actors seeking to destabilise the region. Strengthening security cooperation through increased intelligence sharing, joint military exercises, and coordinated maritime security efforts can significantly mitigate these threats. Establishing regional security mechanisms and joint capacity-building programmes in combating violent extremism can enhance member nations' readiness and response capabilities, fostering a collective security approach.

4. Climate Change and Environmental Concerns:

Climate change poses a global challenge requiring collective action. BRICS+ and the GCC must prioritise collaboration on climate change adaptation and mitigation measures and sustainable development. Sharing expertise on renewable energy technologies, promoting green financing, and facilitating joint research projects can help member countries effectively address environmental concerns while creating shared economic and environmental benefits. Collective advocacy for international agreements like the Paris Agreement can also demonstrate a unified commitment to combating climate change.

5. Technological Advancements:

The rapidly advancing technological landscape presents both opportunities and challenges for BRICS+ and the GCC. Collaboration in emerging technologies, such as artificial intelligence, blockchain, and renewable energy, can fuel economic growth and innovation. Establishing technology transfer programmes, promoting research and development partnerships, and facilitating entrepreneurship and start-up ecosystems can enable member nations to harness the benefits of technological advancements. Bridging the digital divide within the consortiums should also become a priority to ensure equitable access to technological opportunities.

6. Cultural and Linguistic Barriers:

Cultural diversity and linguistic variations can sometimes hinder effective communication and understanding among member nations. Promoting cultural exchanges and enhancing people-to-people connections can break down these barriers. Investments in cultural programmes, language learning initiatives, and tourism collaborations can foster mutual understanding, appreciation, and respect for diverse traditions. Cultural festivals, youth exchanges, and educational scholarships can effectively build bridges and forge stronger cultural ties within the consortiums.

Overcoming these challenges demands continuous efforts, adaptability, and a commitment to dialogue and collaboration. BRICS+ and the GCC can establish regular platforms for consultation, such as summits, ministerial meetings, and technical working groups, to build trust, identify common priorities, and promote joint action. A shared vision and strategic planning are crucial to developing comprehensive frameworks that promote inclusive growth, enhance security cooperation, address climate change, embrace technology, and celebrate cultural diversity.

Recognising the need for flexible approaches, tailor-made strategies, and outcome-oriented initiatives, member nations must leverage their strengths, share knowledge, and pool resources. By forging a stronger partnership based on trust, understanding, and resilience, BRICS+ and the GCC can overcome mutual challenges, tap into untapped potential, and create a brighter future for their people while contributing to global prosperity.

19

GEOPOLITICAL IMPLICATIONS: BRICS+, THE GULF, AND THE UNITED STATES

— ◦ —

T his chapter will explore the intricate and evolving relationships between BRICS+, the Gulf Cooperation Council (GCC), and the United States. As the global order undergoes significant changes, it is crucial to analyze the geopolitical consequences of these emerging alliances. This extended version of the chapter will provide a more in-depth exploration of the subject matter, examining the historical context, regional dynamics, and potential future scenarios.

The Role of the United States in the Changing Global Order:

The United States has traditionally occupied a position as the dominant global power, shaping the international landscape by its interests. However, the global power balance has been undergoing a significant transformation in recent years. The rise of BRICS+, an association of emerging markets including Brazil, Russia, India, China, and South Africa, alongside the growing economic importance of the Gulf countries, is challenging the traditional Western dominance. In this new global order, the United States faces the need to adapt its strategies and priorities to maintain its influence and control over global affairs.

US Relations with BRICS+ and the Gulf Countries:

The United States' relationship with BRICS+ and the GCC is multifaceted, encompassing elements of cooperation, competition, and potential conflict areas. The United States has historically maintained robust economic and political ties with these emerging alliances. Despite their enormous economic potential, BRICS+ countries have faced numerous coordination and collective action challenges due to differing political systems, developmental stages, and strategic priorities. Nevertheless, the United States recognises their significance as emerging forces in the global landscape.

Similarly, the Gulf countries, such as Saudi Arabia, the United Arab Emirates, Qatar, and others, have risen in prominence due to their vast oil reserves and strategic geographical location. The United States has long maintained a strong security and economic partnership with these countries to secure energy flows, counter regional threats, and promote stability. However, recent developments, including shifting regional dynamics and the rise of new power centres, have introduced complexities in US-Gulf relations, requiring recalibration of policies and approaches.

Power Struggles and Realignment of Geopolitical Alliances:

The rise of BRICS+ and the growing influence of the Gulf countries are leading to the realignment of global geopolitical alliances. As traditional power structures face new challengers, nations seek to safeguard their interests by forming and reconfiguring alliances. This realignment often leads to power struggles and geopolitical tensions as different nations vie for influence and seek to shape the evolving global order.

For the United States, the emergence of BRICS+ and the Gulf countries poses both opportunities and challenges. On one hand, engaging constructively with these rising powers can help maintain US influence and promote stability. Enhanced economic cooperation, technology sharing, and diplomatic dialogue can facilitate mutual understanding and constructive engagement. On the other hand, increased competition for resources, markets, and geopolitical influence can test the United States' ability to navigate this changing landscape effectively while addressing potential areas of friction.

The Role of BRICS+ and the GCC in Reshaping the Global Political Landscape:

BRICS+ and the GCC collectively possess considerable economic, military, and political influence, which is increasingly shaping the global political landscape. As they continue to strengthen their alliances and assert themselves regionally and globally, they are reshaping the existing norms and institutions, leading to the development of alternative mechanisms.

The BRICS countries have established the New Development Bank and the Contingent Reserve Arrangement, offering alternatives to existing Western-dominated financial institutions like the World Bank and the International Monetary Fund. These initiatives aim to address the concerns of developing countries and promote greater economic independence from the traditional Western-centric financial system. Additionally, BRICS+ countries actively participate in multilateral forums, such as the United Nations and G20, to amplify their voices on global issues and promote a multipolar world order.

On the other hand, the Gulf countries have been working towards regional integration through the GCC, with joint initiatives and organisations in areas such as defence cooperation, economic coordination, and energy policies. The GCC's influence extends beyond its borders, with regional interventions and mediation efforts to shape regional affairs in the Middle East. This assertiveness highlights the Gulf countries' desire to participate more actively in regional and global decision-making processes.

Conclusion:

As geopolitical rivalries intensify and international relations become increasingly complex, the interactions between BRICS+, the Gulf countries, and the United States will significantly shape the future global order. This extended version of the chapter has provided a deeper analysis, examining the historical context, regional dynamics, and potential future scenarios. Understanding the geopolitical implications of these emerging alliances is essential for policymakers and analysts in navigating the evolving global landscape. By staying informed and adaptable, countries can better position themselves to thrive in this changing world.

20

THE ROLE OF THE UNITED STATES IN THE CHANGING GLOBAL ORDER

— ◦ —

T he United States has long been a dominant player in the international arena, shaping the global order through its economic, military, and cultural influence. However, recent years have seen a significant shift in power dynamics, challenging the traditional Western dominance and introducing new players to the global stage. This chapter explores the evolving role of the United States in this changing global order, delving deeper into the economic, military, and cultural aspects of its influence.

One crucial aspect to consider is the economic dimension. The United States has been a vital driver of global economic growth, fuelled by its robust consumer market, technological advancements, and innovation. This economic prowess has allowed the United States to shape global trade agreements, establish multinational corporations, and influence monetary policies. Over the years, the United States has played a pivotal role in fostering economic integration and promoting free trade. Initiatives like the establishment of the World Trade Organisation (WTO) and the signing of bilateral and multilateral trade agreements, such as the North American Free Trade Agreement (NAFTA) and the recently renegotiated United States-Mexico-Canada Agreement (USMCA), have facilitated economic cooperation and market access. However, the rise of emerging economies within BRICS+ and other regional alliances has introduced new economic competitors, offering alternative economic growth and development visions. China, in particular, has emerged as a significant economic powerhouse, challenging American hegemony in various sectors, from manufacturing to technology. This shift in economic power has altered trade dynamics and created competition for resources and markets. The United States now finds itself navigating a more complex and interconnected global economic landscape, where collaboration, negotiation, and adaptability are paramount. As the United States seeks to maintain its economic influence, it must balance protecting its domestic industries, addressing economic inequalities, and embracing a more multilateral approach that reflects the changing global economic realities.

In addition to economic dynamics, the United States has played a crucial role in maintaining global security and stability. As the world's leading military power, the United States has been involved in numerous conflicts and peacekeeping operations, shaping the global security architecture. Its military alliances, such as NATO, have ensured collective defence and deterrence against potential adversaries. The United States has also pursued non-proliferation efforts, arms control agreements, and promoting the development of international institutions such as the United Nations. However, the changing global order has necessitated a reevaluation of strategic priorities. With the rise of non-Western powers and the emergence of new security challenges, such as cyber warfare and terrorism, the United States has had to adapt its military and security strategies. This includes shifting focus and resources towards addressing new asymmetric threats, emphasising intelligence cooperation, and engaging in diplomatic initiatives to diffuse tensions. The United States continues to assert its military presence and influence but must do so within the context of this evolving global order. Additionally, the United States has recognised the importance of strategic competition in emerging domains such as space and cyberspace, investing in technological advancements to ensure its edge in these areas. This transformation requires the United States to maintain partnerships and alliances, share intelligence, and adapt its military capabilities to address regional and global security challenges effectively.

Furthermore, the United States has been a vocal advocate for democratic values, human rights, and the rule of law. It has often used its influence and soft power to promote these ideals on the global stage, supporting democratic movements, advocating for international human rights standards, and defending the principles of free speech and freedom of the press. Building on its own democratic institutions and experiences, the United States has actively promoted democracy and political stability worldwide. However, the changing dynamics of the global order have given rise to new political alliances and ideologies, some diverging from Western democratic norms. The rise of authoritarian regimes and illiberal democracies challenges the universal application of Western ideals. The United States now faces the challenge of navigating these different political landscapes and finding common ground with emerging powers that may have different political systems and values. This requires engaging in dialogue, building diplomatic relationships, and promoting shared interests and objectives. The United States recognises the importance of fostering cooperation with non-Western powers, seeking areas of collaboration on issues such as climate change, global health, and counterterrorism while continuing to advocate for democratic values. Moreover, by maintaining strong relationships with its traditional allies, the United States can sustain its influence and work collectively toward shaping a more inclusive and responsive global order.

In this changing global order, the role of the United States has become more complex and multifaceted. It must navigate shifting economic power dynamics, reevaluate its military strategies, and engage with diverse political ideologies. The United States has a stake in shaping the global order to align with its key interests, such as promoting free and fair trade, preserving national security, and upholding democratic values. As the global order continues to evolve, the United States needs to adapt its policies and strategies accordingly while finding opportunities for collaboration and cooperation with emerging powers and alliances like BRICS+. This will not only shape the United States' role in the changing global order but also contribute to shaping the future trajectory of the international system as a whole. The United States holds great potential to leverage its economic, military, and cultural influence to promote stability, peace, and prosperity in this ever-changing world.

21

US RELATIONS WITH BRICS+ AND THE GULF COUNTRIES

— ◦ —

A s the global order continues to shift, the United States navigates its relationships with the BRICS+ consortium and the Gulf Cooperation Council (GCC). These relationships are crucial in determining the balance of power and influence in the evolving geopolitical landscape.

The United States has traditionally been a dominant force in global affairs. However, with the rise of the BRICS+ countries – Brazil, Russia, India, China, South Africa, and additional emerging economies – and the economic and strategic importance of the Gulf countries, the United States must adapt its approach to maintain its position.

US relations with BRICS+ countries have been multifaceted and have evolved over time. On one hand, the United States has recognised these emerging powers' economic potential and sought to engage them in trade and investment. Economic cooperation and integration have been at the forefront of US-BRICS+ relations, with efforts such as the Trans-Pacific Partnership (TPP) and the Regional Comprehensive Economic Partnership (RCEP) being central to these initiatives.

The BRICS+ countries, with their combined population of over 3 billion people and growing middle class, present significant opportunities for US exporters and investors. American companies have increasingly looked to these emerging economies for market expansion, capitalising on their consumer-driven economic growth. Additionally, the United States recognises the need to cultivate deeper institutional ties with these countries to strengthen regional stability and promote a rules-based international order.

While economic cooperation has been a significant aspect of US-BRICS+ relations, there have also been challenges and disagreements on various fronts. Intellectual property rights protection remains a contentious issue. The United States has expressed concerns over copyright infringement, unfair trade practices, and technology transfer. These concerns hinder closer cooperation, as protecting intellectual property rights is necessary for fostering innovation and ensuring a level playing field in the global marketplace.

Market access barriers also impede the United States' quest for fair competition in these emerging markets. Non-tariff barriers, such as onerous regulations and bureaucratic red tape, continue to pose challenges for American businesses seeking entry into BRICS+ markets. However, the United States has been actively negotiating to address these barriers and promote greater market access for American companies.

Moreover, human rights concerns have strained relations between the United States and BRICS+ countries. The United States has consistently advocated for democratic governance, civil liberties, and individual freedoms. Differences in political systems and values between the United States and these countries have sometimes led to friction, particularly regarding freedom of expression, human rights abuses, and religious freedom. Balancing these concerns while maintaining constructive engagement is key to fostering productive relationships.

China's prominent membership in both BRICS+ and the Gulf countries' economic landscape further complicates US relations. The United States has recognised the need to compete and cooperate strategically with China. It acknowledges the importance of maintaining a healthy level of competition to safeguard its economic interests and technological advancements, particularly in sectors such as advanced manufacturing, artificial intelligence, and 5G networks.

Simultaneously, the United States recognises the importance of cooperation in areas of shared concern. Addressing global challenges, such as climate change, public health crises, and the non-proliferation of weapons of mass destruction, necessitates collaboration among major powers, including China. Strategic engagement with China on common issues can contribute to global stability and address pressing challenges that transcend national borders.

Turning to US relations with the Gulf Cooperation Council, these have traditionally been long-standing and primarily driven by strategic interests. For decades, the United States has been a key partner in ensuring the security and stability of the Gulf region.

This partnership has involved military support, arms sales, and cooperation in countering terrorism.

The United States' military presence in the Gulf has been marked by establishing military bases, joint exercises, and security cooperation agreements. These efforts aim to deter aggression, promote stability, and safeguard international energy flows. The presence of US forces in the region has acted as a deterrent against external threats, including those posed by Iran while ensuring the security of key sea lanes and trade routes.

However, recent geopolitical developments have added new complexities to US-Gulf relations. The Iran nuclear deal, officially known as the Joint Comprehensive Plan of Action (JCPOA), created divisions within the GCC. While some Gulf countries supported the agreement as a means to curb Iran's nuclear ambitions and regional influence, others expressed concerns about its efficacy and the need for addressing broader security concerns in the region.

The subsequent withdrawal of the United States from the JCPOA under the previous administration further strained relations within the region. The renewed tensions between the United States and Iran and the subsequent escalation of regional conflicts have posed challenges to the stability and security of the Gulf. The United States now faces the task of recalibrating its approach and engaging with regional partners to find a comprehensive and sustainable solution to longstanding issues.

Furthermore, the changing dynamics of global energy markets have impacted US-Gulf relations. The United States' increasing domestic oil and gas production, along with the emergence of alternative energy sources, has altered the once-exclusive dependence on Gulf energy resources. The United States has transitioned from a net importer to a net energy exporter, significantly reducing its reliance on Gulf oil supplies.

This shift has led to reevaluating the economic dynamics between the United States and the Gulf countries and a need for greater diversification of their bilateral partnerships. Both sides are exploring new areas of cooperation beyond energy, including investments in infrastructure, technology, education, and healthcare. The United States has sought to leverage its cybersecurity, renewable energy, and innovation expertise to support the Gulf countries in their economic diversification efforts.

Moreover, the United States recognises the importance of aligning its engagement with the Gulf countries with regional dynamics and priorities. While the GCC operates as a collective body in many areas, individual member countries have unique challenges, preferences, and aspirations. Understanding and addressing these specific needs is essential for strengthening partnerships and fostering mutually beneficial outcomes.

In conclusion, US relations with both the BRICS+ consortium and the Gulf countries hold significant implications for the global order. Navigating these relationships requires the United States to adapt its approach, recognising the evolving power dynamics and the need for constructive engagement. Prioritising economic cooperation, promoting fair market access, protecting intellectual property rights, and addressing human rights concerns are essential to fostering meaningful partnerships with BRICS+ countries.

In the Gulf region, maintaining strategic stability, addressing regional security concerns, and diversifying bilateral partnerships beyond energy are key considerations for the United States. Balancing the interests of different Gulf countries, engaging in diplomatic efforts, and seeking common ground to address challenges and promote stability is crucial.

Success in managing these relationships will significantly influence the balance of power and shape the future trajectory of global affairs. The United States must demonstrate strategic thinking, flexibility, and adaptability to navigate the complexities of the world stage, thereby securing its interests and achieving mutually beneficial outcomes with these key players.

22

POWER STRUGGLES AND REALIGNMENT OF GEOPOLITICAL ALLIANCES

— ◆ —

In the past few years, there have been significant changes in the global order, marked by power struggles and realignment of geopolitical alliances. This chapter delves into the complex dynamics of these changes, examining the evolving role of the United States, the emergence of the BRICS+ consortium, and the growing influence of the Gulf Cooperation Council (GCC) in shaping the new global landscape.

The United States, long considered the world's superpower, navigates a shifting geopolitical paradigm. As the BRICS+ countries (Brazil, Russia, India, China, South Africa, and the potential addition of other nations) rise as emerging powers, America's dominance in global affairs is reevaluated. This chapter unveils the implications of these changes for the United States and its role as it seeks to assert its influence and maintain its position in this transformed era.

US relations with the BRICS+ consortium and the Gulf countries are multifaceted and complex. While the BRICS+ group collectively challenges American hegemony, individual alliances within this consortium vary widely. China, in particular, has emerged as a formidable competitor to the United States, challenging its economic supremacy and promoting an alternative vision of global governance. Beyond its robust economic growth, China has been expanding its influence through initiatives like the Belt and Road Initiative (BRI) and the Asian Infrastructure Investment Bank (AIIB), which aim to create new economic corridors and establish institutions beyond the existing framework dominated by the West. Conversely, Russia seeks to exert its influence through strategic partnerships and geopolitical interventions, often using energy resources as a diplomatic tool. India and Brazil, aiming to solidify their regional dominance, often find themselves balancing between allegiance to the existing global order and pursuing their national interests. Their evolving relationships with the United States and other major powers significantly influence the geopolitical landscape.

Meanwhile, the GCC presents unique opportunities and challenges for the United States. In addition to strong economic ties, the United States maintains crucial security partnerships with Gulf countries. However, geopolitical dynamics in the region have shifted, especially due to the ongoing rivalry between Saudi Arabia and Iran, the rise of non-state actors like ISIS, and the complexities of the Arab Spring aftermath. This chapter further explores how the United States balances its strategic interests with the complexities of regional conflicts, sectarian tensions, and the aspirations of the Gulf nations. It examines American efforts to strengthen regional security mechanisms, including arms sales, military partnerships, and counterterrorism cooperation. Understanding the intricate dynamics between the United States and the GCC is essential to comprehending the broader Middle Eastern landscape.

Given these power shifts, traditional geopolitical alliances also undergo significant realignments. This chapter analyses the changing dynamics among major powers, such as the United States, China, Russia, India, Brazil, and the GCC countries. It assesses the motivations and strategies driving these realignments, whether rooted in economic interests, ideological compatibility, or the pursuit of regional hegemony. Exploring the complexities of these changing alliances, including the impact of historical rivalries, territorial disputes, and resource competition, enhances our understanding of the nuances shaping contemporary global politics and security.

Moreover, the rising influence of the BRICS+ consortium and the GCC enacts a profound reshaping of the global political landscape. The ability to reshape international norms, governance institutions, and regional security architectures is at stake. This chapter examines the initiatives these emerging powers undertake to assert their influence, such as proposing alternative financial institutions, initiating regional security dialogues, and fostering cultural and economic exchanges. It highlights the challenges these countries face in gaining broader acceptance and overcoming scepticism from established powers, particularly in the context of existing institutions like the United Nations and the World Trade Organisation. Assessing the extent to which these efforts challenge or complement existing power structures informs our understanding of the future of international relations.

In conclusion, power struggles and geopolitical alliances' realignments have precipitated a global order's seismic shift. This extended chapter provides a comprehensive analysis of these transformations, shedding light on the changing dynamics for the United States, the rise of the BRICS+ consortium, and the growing influence of the GCC. By exploring the intricacies of these relationships, readers gain a deeper understanding of the complexities involved in navigating the new global landscape. The evolving roles of major powers and the initiatives undertaken by emerging economies shape the contours of global politics and set the stage for the future of international relations.

23

THE ROLE OF BRICS+ AND THE GCC IN RESHAPING THE GLOBAL POLITICAL LANDSCAPE

— ◆ —

The world is currently undergoing a significant change in power dynamics, where emerging economies and regional alliances are playing a crucial role in shaping the global political landscape. In this chapter, we explore the importance of the BRICS+ consortium and the Gulf Cooperation Council (GCC) in reshaping global politics and challenging the predominant influence of traditional global powers.

The BRICS+ consortium, comprising Brazil, Russia, India, China, South Africa, and additional partner countries, has solidified its position as a formidable force in the global arena. These nations comprise a substantial share of the world's population, economy, and military capabilities. Over the years, the collective political influence and growing role of BRICS+ in international organisations such as the United Nations, World Trade Organisation, and G20 have further enhanced their impact on important global decision-making processes.

One of the key ways in which BRICS+ is reshaping the global political landscape is through their promotion of multipolarity. Historically dominated by Western powers, global governance institutions have been criticised for their limited representation and exclusionary practices. However, power dynamics are gradually shifting with the rise of BRICS+ and their continued advocacy for a more inclusive and representative global order. These countries challenge Western dominance by strongly advocating for long-overdue reforms in international institutions such as the UN Security Council, aiming to reflect the emerging realities of the world and allow for greater inclusivity.

Moreover, BRICS+ countries are actively pursuing a multipolar global economic order that diversifies the sources of economic growth and influence. Their efforts to establish alternative financial institutions, like the New Development Bank and the Asian Infrastructure Investment Bank, provide platforms for these nations to have a greater say in global economic governance. By offering alternative lending and investment mechanisms, BRICS+ countries challenge the existing financial architecture dominated by traditional global powers, thereby reshaping economic policies and power dynamics.

Furthermore, the BRICS+ countries are fostering closer economic ties among themselves, promoting trade, investment, and technological cooperation. By leveraging their vast consumer markets, natural resources, and manufacturing capabilities, these nations are transforming the balance of economic power and challenging the established global economic order. The Belt and Road Initiative development by China, a massive infrastructure project linking Asia, Europe, and Africa, is a prime example of how BRICS+ countries are reshaping global connectivity and trade patterns. By creating new corridors for commerce and enhancing connectivity, BRICS+ nations are forging new growth and trade pathways that challenge Western economies' traditional dominance.

The Gulf Cooperation Council (GCC), comprising Bahrain, Kuwait, Oman, Qatar, Saudi Arabia, and the United Arab Emirates, has also emerged as a formidable regional alliance that significantly influences global politics. Their strategic location and vast energy resources give the GCC considerable sway in international affairs. As major oil and gas exporters, the GCC countries can impact global energy prices and supply chains, which, in turn, affects the global political landscape as countries must navigate their relationships with the GCC to secure energy resources and ensure economic stability.

Moreover, the GCC's strategic location in the heart of the Middle East positions it as a crucial player in regional security dynamics. The alliance has actively resolved conflicts, mediation efforts, humanitarian initiatives, and counterterrorism campaigns within the Middle East. By exerting their influence in regional affairs, the GCC countries contribute to reshaping the global political landscape, as the stability and security of the Middle East have far-reaching consequences on global peace and security.

The convergence of BRICS+ and the GCC in reshaping the global political landscape is driven by shared interests and a desire to challenge the existing power structures. Both alliances strive for a more equitable and just global order that accurately reflects the multipolar realities of the 21st century. This convergence can significantly challenge Western powers' traditional dominance, leading to more inclusive decision-making processes, comprehensive reforms in global governance, and a rebalancing of economic power.

In addition, the BRICS+ and GCC alliances are increasingly collaborating and strengthening their ties. Recognising their shared perspectives on multipolarity and the need for a more balanced global order, BRICS+ and GCC countries have initiated dialogues, joint forums, and trade agreements to deepen their cooperation. These collaborations enhance their capabilities and amplify their collective voice when advocating for reforms and addressing global challenges.

It is important to highlight that the BRICS+ and GCC alliances face their own domestic and regional challenges as they navigate their paths towards emerging global powers. Issues such as development disparities, geopolitical rivalries, and internal political dynamics pose hurdles. However, their concerted efforts to address these challenges and find common ground underline the determination to reshape the global political landscape in a way that reflects the evolving multipolarity of the world.

In conclusion, the role of BRICS+ and the GCC in reshaping the global political landscape cannot be underestimated. Their growing influence, both individually and collectively, poses a substantial challenge to the dominance of traditional global powers. Through their relentless promotion of multipolarity, persistence in advocating for reforms in global governance, proactive engagement in regional and global affairs, and deepening collaboration, these alliances actively contribute to a more balanced, equitable, and inclusive global political order. Policymakers and stakeholders must closely monitor and actively engage with this ongoing transformation to navigate the opportunities and challenges it presents.

24

STRATEGIC AND ECONOMIC CONVERGENCE BETWEEN BRICS+ AND GULF COOPERATION COUNCIL

— • —

As the global geopolitical landscape continues to evolve, the convergence of interests between the BRICS+ consortium and the Gulf Cooperation Council (GCC) has become increasingly important. This chapter explores this convergence's strategic and economic dimensions, highlighting the potential for enhanced cooperation and mutually beneficial outcomes.

1. Security Cooperation and Military Capabilities:

The convergence of interests between the BRICS+ countries and the Gulf Cooperation Council (GCC) region in terms of security cooperation and military capabilities offers significant potential for collaboration. Both BRICS+ countries (including Brazil, Russia, India, China, and South Africa) and GCC countries possess substantial military strength and strategic interests that align with the security concerns of the Gulf region. Joint military exercises, intelligence sharing, and capacity-building initiatives can be pursued to enhance stability and security and address common challenges such as piracy, maritime security, and non-traditional security threats like cyber warfare and hybrid warfare.

The GCC countries have expressed interest in diversifying their defence partnerships beyond traditional allies in recent years. BRICS+ countries, on the other hand, are seeking to expand their influence and collaborations in various regions of the world. This convergence in defence interests allows joint research and development initiatives, military technology transfers, and the establishment of defence-industrial cooperation. Collaboration in missile defence systems, naval capabilities, and counterterrorism capabilities can significantly strengthen the security architecture in both regions.

2. Counterterrorism Efforts and Regional Security Challenges:

The BRICS+ countries and the GCC face common security threats related to radicalisation, extremism, and terrorism. In light of this, there is potential for greater cooperation in intelligence sharing, border control measures, and coordinated counterterrorism initiatives. Sharing best practices, conducting joint operations, and establishing regional counter-terrorism centres can significantly contribute to combating terrorism effectively.

Addressing the factors that contribute to radicalisation, such as socioeconomic disparities, exclusion, and ideological manipulation, is crucial in preventing the spread of extremism. BRICS+ and GCC countries can undertake joint development programmes, educational initiatives, and community outreach efforts to address these underlying issues. Both regions can work towards long-term peace and stability by promoting inclusive societies, emphasising religious tolerance, and providing opportunities for youth empowerment.

The convergence of interests in regional security challenges extends beyond counterterrorism efforts. BRICS+ and the GCC can also cooperate in addressing non-traditional security threats, such as cybersecurity, climate change, drug trafficking, and human trafficking. Sharing expertise, exchanging information, and coordinating efforts can strengthen the capacity of both regions to respond to these challenges effectively.

3. Infrastructure Development and Connectivity Initiatives:

Infrastructure development and connectivity initiatives offer another area of strategic convergence between BRICS+ and the GCC. Both regions have ambitious plans for infrastructure development, including transportation networks, energy corridors, and digital connectivity. Capitalising on their economic strengths and expertise, BRICS+ and GCC countries can engage in joint infrastructure projects that enhance regional connectivity, facilitate trade, and promote economic growth.

The establishment of transport and logistics networks, such as the Belt and Road Initiative, Moscow-Kazan High-Speed Railway, Trans-Arabian Railway, and GCC transportation projects, can provide greater access to markets, fostering economic integration and allowing for the efficient movement of goods and services. Moreover, investing in digital infrastructure, including broadband connectivity and e-commerce platforms, can enhance digital connectivity and promote the growth of digital economies in both regions.

4. Economic Collaboration and Trade:

From an economic standpoint, the potential for strategic convergence between BRICS+ and the GCC is significant. BRICS+ countries are some of the fastest-growing economies in the world and offer immense market potential. GCC countries possess substantial financial resources and have demonstrated their ability to invest in diverse sectors globally. By leveraging these complementary strengths, BRICS+ and the GCC can explore opportunities for trade and investment, technology transfers, and joint ventures across sectors such as energy, manufacturing, technology, agriculture, and infrastructure.

To facilitate trade and investment, reducing trade barriers, harmonising regulations, and establishing preferential trade agreements can be explored. Encouraging collaborations between small and medium-sized enterprises (SMEs) in both regions can also promote innovation and entrepreneurship. Furthermore, leveraging their collective economic power, BRICS+ and the GCC can work towards establishing a more balanced and inclusive global economic order through reforms of existing global financial institutions and greater cooperation among emerging markets to address financial challenges and promote sustainable economic growth.

5. Energy Collaboration and Sustainability:

Collaboration in the energy field holds great potential for both BRICS+ and the GCC.

BRICS+ countries, including Russia and China, are major energy consumers, while the GCC countries are significant oil and gas suppliers. Both regions can benefit from secure and sustainable energy supplies by forging strategic energy partnerships, such as long-term supply agreements, joint exploration and development initiatives, and cooperation in renewable energy technologies.

Moreover, leveraging expertise in clean energy technologies can help transition towards a more sustainable and environmentally friendly landscape while addressing global energy challenges such as climate change. With their collective investment capabilities and technological advancements, BRICS+ and the GCC can undertake joint research and development projects, promote technology transfers, and establish clean energy cooperation platforms to accelerate the adoption of renewable energy sources and reduce carbon emissions.

6. Cultural Diplomacy and People-to-People Exchanges:

The convergence between BRICS+ and the GCC goes beyond strategic and economic aspects. Cultural diplomacy and people-to-people exchanges can be crucial in fostering deeper ties between the regions. By promoting cultural understanding, educational exchanges, tourism, and intercultural dialogue, BRICS+ and the GCC can strengthen their relationships at the grassroots level, fostering a sense of trust, cooperation, and mutual respect.

Both regions have rich cultural heritages, diverse traditions, and vibrant arts. Collaborative cultural events, festivals, and exhibitions can be organised to showcase the cultural assets of each region, fostering a deeper appreciation and understanding among the people. Furthermore, educational exchange programmes, scholarships, and academic collaborations can facilitate the transfer of knowledge and expertise, nurturing the next generation of leaders and fostering cross-cultural collaboration in various fields.

Conclusion:

The strategic and economic convergence between BRICS+ and the Gulf Cooperation Council holds immense potential for both regions. By capitalising on shared security concerns, infrastructure development plans, economic strengths, energy collaboration, and cultural exchanges, they can forge robust partnerships that contribute to regional stability, economic development, and a more balanced and inclusive global order.

Recognising the opportunities presented by this convergence, stakeholders in both regions must work towards harnessing their full potential to benefit their respective countries and the international community. By investing in closer cooperation in security, counterterrorism efforts, infrastructure development, economic collaboration, energy sustainability, and cultural diplomacy, BRICS+ and the GCC can establish a durable strategic partnership framework that enhances regional peace, stability, and prosperity.

25

SECURITY COOPERATION AND MILITARY CAPABILITIES OF BRICS+ AND THE GULF COUNTRIES

— • —

I n this chapter, we will explore the security cooperation and military capabilities of the BRICS+ consortium and the Gulf Cooperation Council (GCC). It is essential to understand their defence strategies and collaborative efforts to comprehend how these nations have been shaping the global security landscape.

The BRICS+ countries, including Brazil, Russia, India, China, South Africa, and potential partner nations, have recognised the importance of enhancing their defence capabilities to protect their national interests and contribute to global stability. These emerging economies continue to experience significant economic growth, and as a result, their military investments and advancements reflect their evolving roles on the international stage.

Brazil, the largest country in South America, plays a pivotal role in regional security and has proactively sought to modernise its military capabilities. Brazil's defence strategy focuses on projecting power in its maritime territory, protecting its Amazon rainforest, and participating in peacekeeping operations. The country seeks international collaboration by joining naval exercises, hosting joint military drills, and engaging in technology transfers. Moreover, Brazil actively promotes cooperation within the BRICS+ framework to foster regional stability and address common security challenges.

With its vast territorial expanse and military tradition, Russia has been asserting itself on the global stage through military strength and diplomatic assertiveness. The country invests heavily in its military to ensure its security interests are protected, and it has demonstrated its capabilities through interventions in Syria and Ukraine. Russia's defence strategy includes the development of advanced weaponry, military drills, and strategic partnerships with countries like India and China. Additionally, Russia actively supports the BRICS+ consortium's security initiatives, such as joint naval exercises and information-sharing mechanisms.

With its diverse security challenges, India has been steadily increasing its defence capabilities to protect its territorial integrity and project power in the Indian Ocean region. India's defence strategy has evolved to modernise its armed forces, strengthen its nuclear deterrence, and develop maritime capabilities. The country actively participates in military exercises, such as the Malabar Exercise with the United States and Japan, to enhance interoperability and regional security. India also actively engages with the BRICS+ consortium to address common security concerns, including counterterrorism and cybersecurity.

With its rapidly growing economy and expanding global interests, China has significantly increased its defence spending, leading to substantial advancements in its military capabilities. China's defence strategy is safeguarding its sovereignty, territorial integrity, and maritime interests. The country has invested in modernising its armed forces with advanced technologies, including cyber warfare capabilities, anti-access/area denial systems, and aircraft carriers. China actively engages in security cooperation within the BRICS+ framework, contributing to joint exercises and research and development projects that enhance regional stability.

South Africa, the sole representative from the African continent in the BRICS+ consortium, emphasises peacekeeping operations, diplomacy, and regional stability in its defence strategy. South Africa is critical to African security by contributing troops to United Nations peacekeeping missions and regional stabilisation initiatives. It actively engages in defence cooperation within the BRICS+ framework to enhance regional security and address challenges emerging from conflicts on the African continent.

Similarly, the Gulf countries have also emphasised security cooperation and military modernisation due to their unique geopolitical circumstances. Their geographical proximity to conflict-prone regions, such as the ongoing conflicts in Syria and Yemen, and their substantial energy reserves have accentuated the need for a robust defence infrastructure.

As a leading member of the GCC, Saudi Arabia has a comprehensive defence strategy focused on safeguarding its borders, protecting its oil infrastructure, and maintaining regional stability. The country invests heavily in advanced weapon systems, including aircraft, missile defence, and naval capabilities. Saudi Arabia actively engages in security cooperation with other Gulf countries through bilateral and multilateral military exercises, intelligence sharing, and joint operations to counter common security threats, such as terrorism and ballistic missile proliferation.

Other GCC countries, including the United Arab Emirates, Qatar, Kuwait, Bahrain, and Oman, have also prioritised the development of their military capabilities. The UAE, for instance, has actively invested in its air force and navy to project power and protect its interests in the region. Qatar has focused on building up its strategic partnerships and hosting international military bases, providing a platform for collective defence efforts. Kuwait, Bahrain, and Oman emphasise regional security cooperation, participating in joint exercises and contributing to international peacekeeping missions.

One crucial aspect of security cooperation among the BRICS+ and the Gulf countries is the collaboration in the defence industry. Recognising the benefits of sharing expertise, resources, and technologies, they aim to develop their defence industries, thereby reducing dependency on external suppliers. Joint research and development projects, arms trade agreements, and military training programmes have been established to foster trust and strengthen their defence capabilities.

Counterterrorism efforts also form an integral part of security cooperation for both the BRICS+ and the GCC countries. These regions have faced significant threats from various terrorist organisations and have recognised the need for cooperative measures. Intelligence sharing, joint military operations, and capacity-building programmes have been initiated to combat terrorism and ensure regional stability. For example, the BRICS countries have established the BRICS Counter-Terrorism Cooperation Working Group to coordinate their efforts in combating terrorism.

Furthermore, the BRICS+ consortium and the Gulf countries have invested in enhancing their military capabilities through modernisation programmes and procuring advanced defence systems. Significant advancements have been witnessed in cyber warfare, unmanned aerial vehicles (UAVs), and naval capabilities. These investments strengthen their own defence capabilities and enable them to contribute to global security efforts, such as participating in peacekeeping missions under the United Nations (UN) mandates.

While security cooperation among the BRICS+ and the Gulf countries bears immense potential, several challenges need addressing. Divergent strategic priorities, historical rivalries, and the presence of non-state actors may pose hurdles in achieving a seamless cooperation framework. However, these challenges can be mitigated through open dialogue, diplomacy, and concerted efforts to address shared security concerns, enabling fruitful cooperation.

It is also important to acknowledge that bilateral and multilateral security cooperation between the BRICS+ and the GCC countries extends beyond the defence sector. Economic cooperation, information sharing, and diplomatic initiatives are crucial in strengthening overall regional security. Platforms like the BRICS summits and the GCC Annual Summits serve as forums for leaders to discuss and coordinate security-related issues, fostering greater understanding and collaboration.

Overall, the security cooperation and military capabilities of the BRICS+ consortium and the Gulf countries play significant roles in shaping regional and global security dynamics. As these nations continue to assert themselves internationally, understanding their defence strategies and collaborative efforts becomes critical for policymakers and analysts alike, ensuring a safer and more stable world for all.

26

COUNTERTERRORISM EFFORTS AND REGIONAL SECURITY CHALLENGES

—— ● ——

C ounterterrorism has become paramount for regional alliances like BRICS+ (Brazil, Russia, India, China, and South Africa, along with its dialogue partners) and the Gulf Cooperation Council (GCC). As the threat of terrorism and extremist ideologies continues to rise, it is imperative to establish concerted efforts to maintain regional security. This chapter delves deeper into the counterterrorism initiatives undertaken by these alliances, addressing regional security challenges, collaborative strategies, evolving dynamics of terrorism, and recommendations for enhanced cooperation.

Counterterrorism Efforts by BRICS+:

The BRICS+ consortium acknowledges the diverse security challenges its member countries face, including regional conflicts, homegrown terrorism, and cross-border threats. Adopting a collaborative approach, BRICS+ has introduced measures to address these challenges and foster collective security. The chapter highlights the key role played by platforms such as the BRICS Joint Working Group on Counter-Terrorism, the BRICS Counter-Terrorism Action Plan, and the BRICS Information Technology Cooperation in effectively addressing conventional and emerging threats.

Intelligence-Sharing and Coordination:

Intelligence-sharing serves as a vital pillar of counterterrorism efforts. Recognising this, BRICS+ countries have devised mechanisms to enhance intelligence cooperation, bolster coordination, and facilitate timely and accurate information exchange. Collaborative frameworks like the BRICS Information Exchange on Counter-Terrorism, the establishment of specialised units focusing on intelligence sharing, and joint training programmes have been instrumental in strengthening intelligence coordination. However, challenges linger, including trust-building, national interest protection, and information security. The chapter explores these challenges in-depth and suggests measures to enhance trust and information sharing among member countries.

Joint Military Operations and Exercises:

BRICS+ member states have recognised the importance of joint military operations and exercises in building operational capabilities and enhancing counterterrorism efforts. These exercises facilitate the exchange of best practices, promote interoperability, and help standardise procedures to develop a cohesive and effective response to terrorism. The chapter delves into the successful joint military exercises of BRICS+ countries, such as the BRICS Anti-Terrorism Exercise and the Shanghai Cooperation Organisation's Peace Mission Series. It analyses these exercises' achievements and challenges, emphasising the significance of continued joint training and exercises in improving counterterrorism capabilities.

Cybersecurity and Countering Online Radicalisation:

In an era of technological advancements, cyber threats and online radicalisation have gained prominence in the global counterterrorism landscape. BRICS+ countries recognise the need to tackle these emerging challenges effectively and have taken significant steps toward enhancing cybersecurity cooperation. The chapter delves deeper into the initiatives undertaken by BRICS+ to address cybersecurity concerns, combat online radicalisation, and ensure safe internet usage. Measures such as joint research projects, information sharing, capacity-building efforts, and developing comprehensive cybersecurity strategies are explored in detail.

Regional Security Challenges Faced by the GCC:

The Gulf region faces unique security challenges arising from geopolitical tensions, political instability, and the spread of extremist ideologies. The chapter delves into these challenges, including the rise of non-state actors, sectarian divisions, regional conflicts, and the influence of external actors. Analysing the GCC's response to maintaining regional security, it explores efforts such as developing the Gulf Integrated Defence Pillar and establishing the Joint Counter-Terrorism Centre. The chapter provides an in-depth analysis of the complexities and nuances of regional security challenges faced by the GCC.

Collaboration and Convergence between BRICS+ and the GCC:

Despite operating in distinct geopolitical contexts, BRICS+ and the GCC share common security concerns and potential areas for collaboration. The chapter assesses the existing mechanisms for cooperation between these regional alliances, such as bilateral agreements, joint exercises, and intelligence-sharing platforms. It analyses the potential for convergence in countering terrorism, highlighting the need for enhanced cooperation, information exchange, and joint capacity-building initiatives. By fostering stronger collaboration, BRICS+ and the GCC can effectively form a robust regional network to address shared security challenges.

Evolving Dynamics of Terrorism and Implications:

Terrorism is an ever-changing phenomenon, constantly adapting to exploit new trends and vulnerabilities. The chapter explores evolving dynamics such as the use of social media for recruitment, the threat of lone-wolf attacks, the challenges posed by the return of foreign fighters, and the nexus between terrorism and organised crime. It emphasises the importance of effectively adapting counterterrorism strategies to address these emerging threats. The chapter also delves into preventive measures, rehabilitation programmes, and deradicalization efforts as crucial to countering extremism and terrorism.

Challenges and Limitations:

The following chapters discuss the challenges and limitations faced by BRICS+ and the GCC in their counterterrorism efforts. These challenges include varying national interests, the lack of agreement on the definition of terrorism and extremism, financial and logistical obstacles, and border security issues. The analysis highlights the importance of addressing these challenges and promoting regional and international cooperation to strengthen counterterrorism efforts more effectively. By overcoming these challenges, BRICS+ and the GCC can create an environment that promotes robust and sustainable regional security.

Conclusion and Future Directions:

The conclusion consolidates the chapter's key findings, emphasising the importance of ongoing cooperation between BRICS+ and the GCC in tackling terrorism. It underscores the need for a comprehensive approach that combines military, intelligence, economic, and social measures to address the root causes of terrorism effectively. The recommendations focus on strengthening multilateral organisations, deepening cross-regional cooperation, fostering dialogue, and promoting capacity-building initiatives to achieve sustainable regional security. By addressing both conventional and emerging threats, BRICS+ and the GCC can contribute significantly to global stability and counterterrorism efforts.

In the face of evolving threats and complex regional dynamics, it remains critical for BRICS+ and the GCC to strengthen their counterterrorism efforts and collaborate effectively. Through a comprehensive and coordinated approach, these alliances have the potential to combat terrorism, safeguard regional security, and make significant contributions to global stability and peace.

27

INFRASTRUCTURE DEVELOPMENT AND CONNECTIVITY INITIATIVES

— • —

Infrastructure development enhances economic growth, promotes trade, and fosters regional integration. In this chapter, we will delve deeper into the infrastructure development and connectivity initiatives undertaken by the BRICS+ consortium and the Gulf Cooperation Council (GCC) countries, exploring their significance, challenges, and potential for collaboration.

The BRICS+ countries, consisting of Brazil, Russia, India, China, and South Africa, alongside their partner countries, have recognised the importance of infrastructure development as a catalyst for economic growth and poverty reduction. These nations have invested heavily in infrastructure projects such as roads, railways, airports, ports, and energy facilities. One of the prime examples of such infrastructure initiatives is China's Belt and Road Initiative (BRI), which aims to enhance connectivity and cooperation through extensive infrastructure development, facilitating the movement of goods, capital, and people across Asia, Europe, and Africa. The establishment of the New Development Bank (NDB) by BRICS countries has also opened up avenues for financing infrastructure projects within the consortium. The NDB focuses on providing funds for sustainable infrastructure and development projects, aligning with the United Nations Sustainable Development Goals.

Similarly, the GCC countries, including Saudi Arabia, the United Arab Emirates, Qatar, Kuwait, Oman, and Bahrain, have made remarkable progress in developing world-class infrastructure, particularly in the transportation and energy sectors. The region has witnessed the construction of state-of-the-art airports, seaports, highways, and railways, significantly contributing to economic development. The GCC nations have invested heavily in developing smart cities, renewable energy projects, and advanced telecommunications networks. It is worth noting that the strategic location of the GCC countries provides them with a substantial advantage in terms of trade and connectivity between Asia, Europe, and Africa.

One area of potential collaboration between the BRICS+ and GCC countries lies in infrastructure investment. Both consortia have immense financial resources and could leverage their investment capabilities to support infrastructure projects in each other's regions. By combining their resources, expertise, and experiences, they can jointly develop infrastructure projects that benefit their own economies and promote regional connectivity. Encouraging private sector participation, promoting public-private partnerships, and utilising innovative financing mechanisms, such as sovereign wealth funds and infrastructure bonds, can enhance the availability of funds for infrastructure development initiatives.

Infrastructure connectivity is another critical aspect that can foster economic integration and trade between the BRICS+ and GCC countries. Enhanced connectivity through cross-border roads, railways, and maritime routes can reduce trade costs, increase market access, and boost economic cooperation among these nations. Establishing transport corridors, such as the Asia-Middle East Initiative, can streamline regional trade and facilitation, enabling efficient movement of goods between the BRICS+ and GCC countries. Moreover, developing integrated logistics networks and trade facilitation measures, such as harmonised customs procedures and simplified regulations, can further enhance connectivity and promote seamless trade flows.

Digital connectivity is becoming increasingly vital in today's global economy. The BRICS+ and GCC countries can collaborate on developing digital infrastructure and connectivity initiatives. Digital infrastructure, including high-speed internet connectivity, data centres, and e-commerce platforms, can facilitate the movement of goods, services, and information across borders. Embracing emerging technologies, such as 5G, artificial intelligence, and blockchain, and promoting digital entrepreneurship and innovation will unlock new opportunities for businesses, entrepreneurs, and consumers in both regions. Establishing digital corridors and cross-border e-commerce platforms can help expand the digital economy and facilitate international trade.

In addition to physical and digital connectivity, energy infrastructure cooperation between the BRICS+ and GCC countries can lead to enhanced energy security and sustainable development. Collaborative development of energy projects, such as gas pipelines, electricity interconnections, and renewable energy installations, can ensure both regions' reliable and diversified energy supply. This will also contribute to global efforts in combating climate change and transitioning to a low-carbon economy. Encouraging technology transfer and knowledge sharing in the energy sector, promoting renewable energy investment, and establishing joint research and development initiatives can drive sustainable energy cooperation between the BRICS+ and GCC countries.

However, it is important to recognise that infrastructure development and connectivity initiatives may face various challenges. These include inadequate funding, regulatory barriers, political differences, and security concerns. Addressing these challenges will require concerted efforts from both the BRICS+ and GCC countries and regional and international institutions. Promoting transparency, streamlining regulatory frameworks, ensuring policy coherence, and establishing dispute resolution mechanisms can help overcome barriers and create an enabling environment for infrastructure development and connectivity.

To promote infrastructure development and connectivity initiatives, the BRICS+ and GCC countries should establish a framework for cooperation and coordination. This could involve sharing best practices, exchanging knowledge and technical expertise, and creating platforms for public-private partnerships. Furthermore, international financial institutions and development agencies should provide support by offering financial resources, technical assistance, and capacity-building programmes. Collaborative efforts between the BRICS+ and GCC countries and international organisations, such as the World Bank, Asian Development Bank, and Islamic Development Bank, can help mobilise resources and reinforce mutual cooperation in infrastructure development.

In conclusion, infrastructure development and connectivity initiatives are key drivers for economic growth, regional integration, and sustainable development. The BRICS+ and GCC countries have the potential to collaborate on various infrastructure projects, enabling them to harness their collective strengths and overcome common challenges. These countries can enhance physical and digital connectivity by working together, fostering energy cooperation, and creating a more integrated and prosperous global order. Strengthening partnerships, promoting investment, and ensuring inclusive and sustainable infrastructure development can pave the way for a brighter future for the BRICS+ and GCC countries and the global community.

28

MUTUAL BENEFITS AND THE POTENTIAL FOR ENHANCED COOPERATION

— ◇ —

In this chapter, we will explore further the potential for collaboration and mutual benefits between the BRICS+ consortium and the Gulf Cooperation Council (GCC). These entities have unique economic strengths and geopolitical positioning that, when utilized effectively, can result in substantial progress in various fields. This will not only benefit the participating nations but also the global community as a whole.

Economic cooperation stands as a primary area of mutual benefit for both the BRICS+ countries and the GCC. The BRICS+ consortium, comprising Brazil, Russia, India, China, South Africa, and other emerging economies, has witnessed rapid economic growth and development in recent years. Collectively, these nations are responsible for a significant portion of global GDP growth. On the other hand, the GCC countries, including Saudi Arabia, the United Arab Emirates, Qatar, Kuwait, Bahrain, and Oman, possess abundant energy resources and substantial financial reserves. By harnessing their respective strengths, collaboration between the BRICS+ consortium and the GCC can establish trade and investment partnerships that benefit both sides and foster balanced economic growth.

Enhancing economic cooperation holds the potential for increased trade volumes and diversification of markets for both BRICS+ and GCC countries. The vast consumer base of the BRICS+ nations presents attractive markets for GCC petroleum and petrochemical exports, while the GCC, as a key supplier of energy resources, can provide stable and secure energy supplies to power the growth of BRICS+ economies. Consequently, such collaborations can contribute to economic stability, improved GDP growth rates, job creation, and enhanced living standards for the populations of both BRICS+ and GCC countries.

Furthermore, there is immense potential for technological partnerships between BRICS+ and the GCC. The BRICS+ countries have made significant strides in science, technology, and innovation, particularly in areas such as renewable energy, advanced manufacturing, biotechnology, and information technology. These nations have heavily invested in research and development, leading to breakthrough technologies that have the potential to revolutionise industries. The ambitious plans for economic diversification and knowledge-based economies of the GCC render them ideal partners to benefit from the technological advancements and expertise of the BRICS+ countries. Collaborations in research and development, knowledge transfer, and joint investment in innovative projects can propel both the BRICS+ consortium and the GCC towards technological advancements, increased economic competitiveness, and sustainable growth.

In addition to economic and technological collaboration, the BRICS+ consortium and the GCC share common security and regional stability challenges. These challenges include terrorism, extremism, and regional conflicts, which transcend national borders and require joint efforts to be effectively addressed. By sharing intelligence, collaborating on counterterrorism efforts, and coordinating security strategies, both entities can significantly contribute to maintaining peace and stability in their respective regions. Additionally, joint military exercises, defence equipment partnerships, and military training programmes can enhance the defence capabilities of both BRICS+ and GCC countries, allowing them to address emerging security threats better and contribute to global peace-keeping efforts.

Infrastructure development and connectivity are essential aspects of collaboration between the BRICS+ consortium and the GCC. The BRICS+ countries have made substantial investments in infrastructure projects such as roads, railways, ports, and telecommunications, aiming to improve connectivity, reduce transportation costs, and enhance regional trade flows. With their strategic geographical location as a bridge between Asia, Africa, and Europe, the GCC countries can serve as vital nodes in the ambitious infrastructure plans of the BRICS+ consortium. Enhancing connectivity through improved trade routes, transportation networks, and digital connectivity can facilitate the movement of goods, services, and people, leading to increased economic integration, cultural exchange, and prosperity for both regions.

Additionally, collaboration in the realm of environmental conservation and sustainability can play a significant role in the partnership between the BRICS+ consortium and the GCC. Both entities face environmental challenges such as climate change, water scarcity, and pollution. The BRICS+ countries and the GCC have increasingly embraced sustainable development practices and invested in renewable energy sources such as solar and wind power. By sharing knowledge, best practices, and technology, they can jointly advance the transition to a green economy, promote clean energy solutions, and mitigate the adverse effects of environmental degradation. Collaborative efforts in environmental conservation, resource management, and climate change adaptation can generate long-term benefits for both regions and contribute to a more sustainable future.

Strong political will, effective diplomatic engagements, and a shared commitment to advancing common goals are essential to fully harness the mutual benefits and potential for enhanced cooperation. As the global order evolves, the successful partnership between the BRICS+ consortium and the GCC has the potential to reshape economic, geopolitical, and environmental dynamics on a global scale. This collaboration can foster a more prosperous and sustainable future for all while also serving as an example of effective collaboration and cooperation for other regions and entities worldwide.

29

IMPLICATIONS FOR THE GLOBAL ORDER

— ◦ —

The Rise of BRICS+ Consortium

Challenging Western Dominance

The BRICS+ consortium, composed of Brazil, Russia, India, China, South Africa, and other partner countries, has emerged as a formidable force challenging the traditional dominance of Western powers in the global order. This section delves deeper into this rise's economic, political, and diplomatic aspects, providing a comprehensive analysis of its impact.

Economically, the growth of the BRICS+ nations has been remarkable over the past few decades. Together, they constitute a significant share of global GDP and have become major players in the international trade arena. Their collective bargaining power in global economic institutions has increased, prompting calls for revising outdated governance structures that no longer reflect the current global economic reality.

Politically, the BRICS+ countries have enhanced their influence on global affairs through diplomatic engagements and strategic alliances. They have intensified efforts to forge new partnerships beyond traditional Western allies, seeking alternative geopolitical and economic alignments. The establishment of the BRICS New Development Bank (NDB) and the Contingent Reserve Arrangement (CRA) has further empowered these nations by providing them with alternative development financing and crisis response mechanisms, challenging the dominance of Western-led institutions.

Moreover, the BRICS+ countries have demonstrated a united front on key global issues such as climate change, global governance reform, and multilateralism. Their collective voice on these matters holds significant weight and suggests a shared vision for reshaping the global order based on equity, inclusivity, and sustainable development principles.

Implications for a Multipolar World

The rise of the BRICS+ consortium signals the emergence of a multipolar world characterised by a more diversified power distribution. This section explores the opportunities and challenges associated with this evolving global landscape.

In terms of opportunities, a multipolar world offers the potential for greater global stability. Decision-making processes may become more inclusive and collaborative with no single dominant power, reducing the likelihood of unilateral actions or hegemonic impositions. It also facilitates increased global trade, investment, and cultural exchange opportunities, fostering economic diversity and interdependence.

However, challenges also arise from the shift towards a multipolar world. Competing interests among the BRICS+ countries may lead to conflicts over resources, spheres of influence, or ideological differences. The restructuring of global institutions to accommodate new power configurations may face resistance from established powers, potentially deepening divisions and creating new fault lines. Also, managing multiple power centres' interplay requires effective cooperation mechanisms and a commitment to multilateralism.

The global order must adapt to these changing dynamics, embracing the opportunities while addressing the challenges to ensure a stable and inclusive multipolar world.

The Influence of the Gulf Cooperation Council (GCC)

Energy Dynamics and Global Economic Stability

The Gulf Cooperation Council, composed of Saudi Arabia, the United Arab Emirates, Qatar, Kuwait, Oman, and Bahrain, has long been a significant player in the global energy market. This section delves into the impact of the GCC's energy policies on global economic stability, exploring its influence and contributions to the global order.

As major oil and gas producers, the GCC countries possess considerable reserves that directly impact energy markets worldwide. Their ability to influence prices, supply volumes, and investment decisions affects both consumers and producers globally. As evident during oil price shocks or regional political tensions, shifts in GCC energy policies can disrupt global economic stability.

Furthermore, the GCC nations have substantially invested in global financial institutions, companies, and infrastructure projects. These investments shape economic interdependencies and give the GCC an influential voice in global economic decision-making, further consolidating its role in the global order.

Geopolitical Realignments and Alliances

This section examines the evolving relationships between the GCC, BRICS+, and the United States, analysing these realignments' dynamics, power struggles, and potential consequences.

Strategic partnerships and collaborations have intensified with growing economic ties between the GCC and BRICS+ countries. These alliances present an increasingly attractive trade, investment, and technological exchange alternative. As a result, the relationships between traditional Western allies, particularly the United States and the GCC, may experience strain as new power dynamics reshape regional and global security arrangements.

The United States, recognising the shifting geopolitical landscape, may adopt different approaches in engaging with the GCC and BRICS+. This may involve renegotiating trade deals, rethinking regional security commitments, or seeking new partnerships to maintain its influence. The impact of these realignments on the existing global order will depend on the responses and strategies employed by all parties involved.

Security Cooperation, Regional Stability, and Connectivity

Countering Terrorism and Ensuring Regional Security

In an era marked by persistent global terrorism threats, this section examines the security cooperation efforts between BRICS+ and the GCC, highlighting their significance in maintaining regional stability and combating terrorism.

Both the BRICS+ consortium and the GCC have made concerted efforts to counter terrorism and address regional security concerns. This includes sharing intelligence, coordinating military operations, and implementing counterterrorism measures. Collaboration in this realm is crucial to ensuring stability within their respective regions and mitigating the spillover effects of terrorism on the global order.

However, successful security cooperation faces challenges stemming from diverse political systems, multilateral rivalries, and historical tensions. Understanding and addressing these challenges through trust-building measures, dialogue, and capacity-building will be vital for sustained progress and the enhancement of regional security architectures.

Infrastructure Development and Connectivity Initiatives

Recognising the importance of infrastructure development and connectivity initiatives, this section explores the efforts of the BRICS+ consortium and the GCC in promoting regional integration, enhancing trade routes, and fostering connectivity across continents.

Initiatives like the Belt and Road Initiative (BRI) and the Gulf rail network aim to improve physical connectivity and build crucial infrastructure across Asia, Africa, and Europe. These endeavours stimulate economic growth, deepen regional interdependencies, and potentially reshape the existing global order by facilitating new trade routes and networks of influence.

However, this connectivity may also lead to geopolitical competition and infrastructural dependencies. Ensuring these projects adhere to sustainable development practises, prioritising local participation, and promoting equitable growth is essential. This approach will be crucial for their long-term success and positive impact on the global order.

Conclusion

In conclusion, the rise of the BRICS+ consortium and the influence of the Gulf Cooperation Council have profound implications for the existing global order. The economic, political, and diplomatic strength of BRICS+ challenges Western dominance and may lead to a multipolar world. The GCC's significant role in global energy dynamics influences economic stability and political alliances. The evolving relationships between the GCC, BRICS+, and the United States, security cooperation efforts, and infrastructure development initiatives further reshape the global order. Acknowledging and understanding these implications is critical for policymakers and stakeholders seeking to navigate the changing dynamics and opportunities arising from these rising alliances and their impact on the global order. Such understanding will enable the formulation of effective strategies to ensure a stable, inclusive, and cooperative global order that addresses the challenges and harnesses the opportunities presented by this changing landscape.

30

THE BRICS+ CONSORTIUM AND ITS IMPACT ON THE WESTERN DOMINANCE

— ● —

The rise of the BRICS+ consortium, consisting of the original BRICS countries (Brazil, Russia, India, China, and South Africa) along with other emerging
economies, is reshaping the global order and challenging the dominance of Western
powers. This chapter explores the implications of the BRICS+ consortium on Western
dominance in various spheres, including economics, politics, culture, and global governance. It highlights key factors driving this impact and the potential outcomes of this
shifting global dynamic.

One of the primary ways in which the BRICS+ consortium challenges Western dominance is through its economic power and influence. The combined GDP of the BRICS+
countries accounts for a significant portion of the global economy, and their growing
consumption and investment patterns are shifting the balance of economic power away
from traditional Western economies. For instance, China's economic strength is driven
by its massive consumer market, technological advancements, and rapid development.
China has become a global economic powerhouse, challenging the Western-dominated
status quo and exerting greater influence on global economic policies, trade alliances, and
investment flows. Similarly, other BRICS+ countries, such as India and Brazil, are also
experiencing significant economic growth and becoming influential players in their respective regions. This economic resurgence enables the BRICS+ countries to shape global
economic agendas, challenge Western-led institutions, and reshape the global economic
landscape.

Furthermore, the BRICS+ countries increasingly assert their positions in international
forums and institutions, such as the United Nations, World Trade Organisation, and
World Bank. Through these platforms, they advocate for reforms that better reflect

the changing global dynamics and represent the interests of emerging economies. The BRICS+ consortium has repeatedly called for the reform and democratisation of global financial institutions better to represent the interests and concerns of developing countries. By challenging Western dominance in these institutions, the BRICS+ countries are pushing for a more equitable global governance system that accommodates the realities and aspirations of emerging economies. In doing so, they seek to dismantle the historically Western-centric decision-making processes and establish a more equitable global order.

Another crucial aspect of the BRICS+ consortium's impact on Western dominance is the diversification of global political alliances. As the BRICS+ countries strengthen their cooperation and develop a shared agenda, they present an alternative narrative to the Western-led liberal order. This alternative narrative emphasises the importance of multipolarity, sovereignty, and non-interference in internal affairs, challenging Western norms and values that have been predominant in global affairs. The BRICS+ consortium promotes a more inclusive approach to global governance, advocating for a world order that respects the diversity of nations, cultures, and developmental paths. This diversification of political alliances challenges the Western-centric geopolitical landscape and paves the way for a more balanced and multipolar global order.

Moreover, the BRICS+ consortium's influence extends beyond economics and politics. The cultural and ideological dimensions play a significant role as well. As the BRICS+ countries gain economic and political power, they also promote their own cultural values and narratives, which differ from the Western-centric worldview. This cultural diversification challenges the dominance of Western culture as the benchmark for global standards and practises, leading to a more multipolar and diverse global order. For example, Chinese cultural influence through media, entertainment, and Confucian values is increasingly expanding its reach, presenting an alternative cultural narrative to that of the West. This growing cultural influence contributes to reshaping global norms and challenges Western-centric cultural hegemony.

It is important to note that the impact of the BRICS+ consortium on Western dominance is not solely about undermining or replacing Western powers. Instead, it highlights a shift towards a more balanced global order, where multiple centres of power coexist and collaborate. The BRICS+ consortium presents an opportunity for cooperation, dialogue, and mutual understanding between Western and non-Western nations, fostering a more inclusive and multipolar world. Acknowledging and valuing the perspectives and contributions of emerging economies can lead to greater stability and prosperity for all nations, creating a more equitable and interconnected global landscape.

In conclusion, the BRICS+ consortium profoundly impacts Western dominance in various spheres, including economics, politics, culture, and global governance. Its growing economic power, increasing influence in international institutions, and alternative narratives challenge the traditional Western-centric global order. The rise of the BRICS+ consortium signals a shift towards a more multipolar world, where emerging economies play a pivotal role in shaping global affairs alongside Western powers. Embracing this changing global dynamic and fostering cooperation between different power centres can ultimately lead to a more balanced, diverse, and prosperous world for all.

31

THE ROLE OF THE GULF COOPERATION COUNCIL IN GLOBAL AFFAIRS

— • —

The Gulf Cooperation Council (GCC) plays an integral and multifaceted role in global affairs. Situated in a region of immense geopolitical significance, the GCC member states – Saudi Arabia, United Arab Emirates, Qatar, Kuwait, Bahrain, and Oman – have emerged as powerful players through their strategic location, vast energy resources, economic influence, and active participation in international organisations.

Foremost, the GCC's energy resources hold immense sway in global affairs. The member states collectively possess approximately 48% of the world's proven oil reserves and 24% of its natural gas reserves. As the largest producer, Saudi Arabia remains a key driver of global oil markets, while Qatar's leading position in LNG exports bolsters its standing in the energy sector. The GCC's ability to control production levels and influence energy prices gives them significant economic leverage, allowing them to shape political landscapes and build strategic relationships worldwide. Consequently, any shifts in GCC energy policies, production rates, or investment decisions can reverberate across global markets, profoundly impacting the economies of other nations and affecting energy security. Its pivotal role in energy diplomacy cannot be underestimated.

Moreover, the GCC's strategic location at the crossroads of major trade routes elevates its significance in global affairs. The Arabian Gulf is a vital maritime pathway connecting Asia, Europe, and Africa. The Strait of Hormuz, flanked by Oman and Iran, is a critical chokepoint through which nearly one-fifth of the world's daily oil shipments pass. The GCC's position allows it to exert considerable influence over the flow of trade, security, and logistics, amplifying its importance in shaping regional and global dynamics. Its pivotal role in maintaining maritime security is essential for ensuring the stability of energy supplies and preserving global trade.

The GCC countries have actively utilised their vast wealth to extend their global influence. Sovereign wealth funds, such as the Public Investment Fund of Saudi Arabia and the Abu Dhabi Investment Authority, have emerged as major players in international financial markets. These funds invest in diverse sectors, including real estate, technology, infrastructure, and renewable energy projects. By diversifying their investment portfolios, the GCC countries seek to reduce reliance on oil revenues, promote economic growth, and forge international partnerships. These financial endeavours have facilitated the establishment of economic ties with countries and corporations worldwide, elevating the GCC's presence across different continents and expanding its sphere of influence.

Furthermore, the GCC engages in multilateral organisations and diplomatic relationships that solidify its role in global affairs. Active participation in global forums such as the United Nations, the Arab League, and the Organisation of Islamic Cooperation amplifies the GCC's voice, enabling it to shape decisions, advocate for its interests, and collaborate on critical global issues. The Council has nurtured strong partnerships with international actors, including the European Union, to foster cooperation in areas ranging from trade and investment to security and technology. By forging alliances with other regional blocs and countries, the GCC expands its influence, promotes dialogue, and builds support for its initiatives.

Security cooperation within the GCC is another essential aspect of its role in global affairs. The Council's commitment to collective security has fostered stability within the region. Establishing the Peninsula Shield Force, a joint military venture exemplifies its dedication to maintaining peace and protecting member states. GCC countries actively contribute troops and resources to international peacekeeping missions and engage in multinational military exercises, displaying their commitment to global security. By actively participating in security initiatives, the GCC enhances its profile and strengthens its influence on security policy at regional and global levels.

However, the GCC's role in global affairs faces various challenges. Internal dynamics within member states, regional conflicts, and geopolitical transitions can disrupt the GCC's unity and influence. The 2017 diplomatic rift between Qatar and some other members illustrated the complexities within the organisation and the potential divisions it may face. Economic diversification and reducing dependence on oil reserves also pose significant challenges that require careful policy planning and implementation. Geopolitical shifts, such as evolving power dynamics in the Middle East or the emergence of new energy sources, can also impact the GCC's position in global affairs. Adapting to these challenges will require maintaining a cohesive vision, promoting solidarity, and forging forward-looking strategies.

In conclusion, the Gulf Cooperation Council is pivotal in global affairs under its strategic location, energy resources, economic influence, and active participation in international organisations. Positioned at the crossroads of major trade routes, the GCC's energy resources and economic initiatives shape global markets, while its active engagement in international forums amplifies its voice and influence in decision-making processes. Moreover, its commitment to collective security and collaboration in regional and global security initiatives underscores its role in fostering stability. As the GCC continues to navigate geopolitical complexities and adapt to global challenges, its ability to engage with stakeholders and advance its interests effectively will be critical in shaping the global order and contributing to a prosperous future for its member states and the wider world.

32

FUTURE SCENARIOS: CONVERGENCE, DIVERGENCE, OR MULTIPOLARITY?

— ⋆ —

I n this chapter, we will explore potential future scenarios that might arise due to the convergence, divergence, or multipolarity between the BRICS+ consortium and the Gulf Cooperation Council (GCC). These scenarios could have significant implications for the global order, international relations, and the balance of power. By thoroughly examining each scenario, including their driving factors, possible outcomes, and associated challenges and opportunities, we aim to provide a comprehensive understanding of the possible future trajectories of BRICS+ and the GCC.

Convergence Scenario:

In the convergence scenario, BRICS+ and the GCC find common ground and align their interests, leading to increased cooperation and collaboration. This convergence could be driven by shared economic goals, such as the desire for increased trade and investment and the establishment of financial mechanisms that reduce reliance on Western-dominated institutions. Furthermore, collaboration on security issues, such as counterterrorism measures and regional stability, could strengthen ties between the two blocs. Additionally, a common vision for global governance, characterised by a more equitable distribution of power, could catalyse partnerships. In this scenario, we can expect the creation of strategic partnerships, joint initiatives, and even a new power bloc that challenges the existing Western dominance in global affairs. BRICS+ and the GCC could work together to enhance regional infrastructure, promote sustainable development, and share technological advancements. They may also collaborate on addressing shared challenges, such as climate change, energy security, and governance issues. However, this convergence would require navigating complex geopolitical dynamics and potential differences in values and priorities. Trust-building measures, cultural exchanges, and diplomatic efforts would be crucial to bridging gaps and establishing a solid foundation for cooperation.

Divergence Scenario:

Alternatively, a divergence scenario may unfold if the interests, priorities, or ideologies of BRICS+ and the GCC significantly diverge. Conflicting economic strategies, political ambitions, or differences in values and principles could lead to separate paths pursued by the two blocs. This divergence may hinder cooperation and collaboration and potentially create new fault lines in the global order. Economic divergences can arise as BRICS+ countries focus on sustainable development, technology-driven industries, and regional integration, while the GCC nations prioritise diversification, energy security, and infrastructure development. Additionally, political divergences may emerge as BRICS+ nations push for multipolar global governance while the GCC remains cautious about the potential dilution of its influence. In this scenario, navigating competing interests and finding common ground would become increasingly challenging, potentially leading to increased competition or even conflicts of interest. Tensions arising from varying approaches to regional security, influence in international institutions, and conflicting alliances could create a fragmented international system. However, despite potential divergence, it is important to note that cooperation on specific issues, such as energy, finance, or counterterrorism, may still be possible, albeit with a narrower focus.

Multipolarity Scenario:

The third possible scenario is the emergence of a multipolar global order, characterised by power distribution among various actors, including BRICS+, the GCC, and other regional powers. Multipolarity entails a more fragmented, decentralised, and complex global system, with multiple power centres exerting influence and shaping global affairs. In this scenario, the global order becomes more fluid, making it necessary to establish new forums, mechanisms, and institutions to manage diverse interests and maintain stability. While multipolarity offers opportunities for increased dialogue, cooperation, and the formation of alliances based on shared interests, it also poses challenges in coordinating policies, resolving conflicts, and addressing global issues collectively. BRICS+ and the GCC, as major players, would aim to shape the evolving international system by promoting multilateralism, advocating for the reform of existing global governance institutions to better reflect the current power distribution, and seeking consensus on pressing global challenges, such as climate change, cyber security, and non-proliferation. Engaging in regional integration efforts, promoting economic interdependence, and fostering cultural exchanges may serve as mechanisms to enhance trust, understanding, and cooperation among diverse powers.

The outcome will depend on the actions and choices of BRICS+ and the GCC, as well as the responses of other global actors, such as the United States and Europe. It is crucial for policymakers, scholars, and global decision-making institutions to analyse and anticipate these potential future scenarios carefully. By doing so, they can proactively shape the global order to ensure stability, promote dialogue, and foster cooperation between BRICS+, the GCC, and other regional and global actors. This entails prioritising diplomacy, engaging in strategic foresight, and fostering an environment of adaptability to changing dynamics. Flexibility, open dialogue, and an understanding of shared interests will be key to navigating these scenarios and forging a future that benefits all stakeholders in the international community.

33

IMPLICATIONS FOR POLICYMAKERS AND GLOBAL
DECISION-MAKING INSTITUTIONS

— ⬩ —

I n this chapter, we will be exploring the significant implications of the emergence of the BRICS+ consortium and the increasing influence of the Gulf Cooperation Council (GCC) on policymakers and global decision-making institutions. The changing power dynamics in the global order call for a comprehensive assessment of the existing frameworks and institutional structures to enable effective navigation of the evolving landscape.

One of the key implications for policymakers is the need to reassess traditional alliances and partnerships in light of the rise of the BRICS+ and the GCC. These emerging regional blocs present exciting opportunities for collaboration and cooperation but also pose challenges as they seek to assert their influence on the global stage. Policymakers must consider the potential benefits and risks of aligning with these powers, considering their geopolitical, economic, and social interests.

The rise of the BRICS+ consortium, comprising Brazil, Russia, India, China, South Africa, and additional emerging economies, has significant economic implications for global trade, investment, and development. These countries hold immense market potential with their combined population of around 3.6 billion people and growing middle classes. Policymakers should actively explore avenues of cooperation with this emerging economic powerhouse, seeking mutually beneficial trade arrangements and investment opportunities. By nurturing economic ties with the BRICS+ countries, policymakers can diversify their countries' economic relationships and tap into new growth opportunities, helping to drive global economic development.

Similarly, the GCC, consisting of Bahrain, Kuwait, Oman, Qatar, Saudi Arabia, and the United Arab Emirates, has become a major economic force due to their vast oil and gas reserves. Policymakers should recognise the significance of these countries' energy resources and ensure energy security in their national and global energy strategies. Collaborative efforts in energy diversification, technology exchange, and investment can support the transition to cleaner and more sustainable energy systems, benefiting the GCC and the world.

Furthermore, the BRICS+ and GCC blocs have geopolitical implications that extend beyond economic considerations. Policymakers must carefully analyse the potential strategic ramifications of the evolving alliances and power dynamics. These regions occupy critical geographic locations, acting as pivotal players in shaping regional security, stability, and conflict resolution efforts. Policymakers should foster open dialogues and diplomatic engagements to mitigate potential risks and foster greater understanding between the existing powers and the emerging players. By engaging in collaborative efforts to address regional conflicts and security threats, policymakers can build trust and develop constructive relations with these emerging powers, promoting peace and stability beyond their respective regions.

Global decision-making institutions, such as international organisations and multilateral fora, must also adapt to accommodate the changing power dynamics. It is essential to reform these institutions to be more inclusive and represent the diverse perspectives and interests of the BRICS+ and GCC countries. Reforms to voting systems, decision-making processes, and leadership positions can help ensure that these institutions adequately reflect the emerging realities of the global order. Embracing the active participation and engagement of the BRICS+ and GCC nations can strengthen global governance and enhance the legitimacy and effectiveness of these institutions in addressing global challenges.

Moreover, policymakers must recognise the potential for increased multipolarity within the global order. The rise of the BRICS+ and the GCC challenges Western countries' traditional dominance and influence. Policymakers should embrace this shift and work towards building a more balanced and inclusive global governance system. This could involve strengthening existing multilateral institutions or creating new platforms for dialogue and cooperation. An inclusive approach will foster cooperation, understanding, and collective responses to global challenges such as climate change, poverty, and security threats.

In conclusion, the implications of the rise of the BRICS+ consortium and the growing influence of the GCC on policymakers and global decision-making institutions are profound. It requires a reassessment of traditional alliances and partnerships, reforming global institutions to accommodate evolving power dynamics, harnessing economic opportunities, evaluating geopolitical repercussions, and embracing a more multipolar global order. By actively engaging with these implications, policymakers can adapt to the changing realities and shape a more equitable and collaborative global governance system that fosters sustainable development and global prosperity.

34

CASE STUDIES: BRICS+-GCC COLLABORATIONS

— ◦ —

Case Study 1: Energy Cooperation and Sustainable Development Initiatives

In this case study, we examine the joint efforts of the BRICS+ consortium and the Gulf Cooperation Council (GCC) in the energy sector. Both BRICS+ and the GCC are significant players in the energy industry, having ample natural resources and high energy requirements. The goal of this partnership is to foster sustainable development, promote energy efficiency, and encourage the use of renewable energy sources.

Over the years, BRICS+ and the GCC have initiated several projects and initiatives to enhance energy cooperation and address environmental challenges. These collaborations have been driven by a shared understanding of the importance of sustainable energy and the need to transition towards a low-carbon future. Energy cooperation between the two regions holds tremendous potential, given their large populations, rapid economic growth, and significant energy resources.

One notable initiative is the establishment of joint research and development ventures in renewable energy technologies. Through collaborative research efforts, both regions have accelerated the development and deployment of renewable energy solutions. This collaboration has resulted in the sharing of knowledge, expertise, and technological advancements, contributing to the growth of the renewable energy sector in both BRICS+ and the GCC.

The joint research and development ventures have focused on various renewable energy sources, such as solar, wind, and bioenergy. For instance, the BRICS+ countries have abundant solar resources, while the GCC countries possess vast deserts with high solar radiation. The collaboration between the two regions has led to the development of more efficient solar panels, innovative solar energy storage solutions, and advanced solar thermal technologies for electricity generation and water desalination.

Simultaneously, wind energy collaboration has flourished due to the BRICS+ countries' vast coastlines and the GCC's potential for wind power generation. Collaborative research has focused on designing efficient wind turbines, exploring offshore wind energy potential, and developing predictive models to maximise wind power utilisation. These advancements have propelled the growth of wind energy installations in both regions, contributing to their sustainable energy portfolios.

Bioenergy collaboration has also proven fruitful for both BRICS+ and the GCC. The BRICS+ consortium, comprising agricultural powerhouses like Brazil and India, has significant expertise in biofuel production from sugarcane and biomass. The GCC, with its substantial agricultural and waste resources, has complementary strengths for bioenergy generation. Collaborative research efforts have focused on enhancing biofuel production processes, utilising food waste and agricultural residues for energy generation, and developing sustainable feedstock cultivation practices.

Another significant aspect of the collaboration is the development of energy efficiency standards. BRICS+ and the GCC have recognised the importance of reducing energy consumption and improving energy efficiency as key strategies for sustainable development. They have worked together to establish common standards and regulations that promote energy-efficient practices across various sectors.

In the transportation sector, the collaboration has led to the development of fuel-efficient vehicles and the promotion of electric vehicle adoption. This has been achieved through joint research and development initiatives, sharing best practices in vehicle design, and establishing charging infrastructure networks. These efforts have reduced greenhouse gas emissions, enhanced energy security, and improved air quality in both regions.

In the construction sector, the collaboration has focused on promoting green building practices and energy-efficient technologies. Joint efforts have resulted in the development of energy-saving building materials, implementing energy management systems, and adopting sustainable design principles. These endeavours have significantly contributed to reducing energy consumption in buildings and lowering carbon footprints.

Furthermore, the exchange of best practices in sustainable energy management has been a crucial component of this collaboration. BRICS+ and the GCC have organised joint workshops, conferences, and training programmes to facilitate sharing experiences and lessons learnt in sustainable energy management. These platforms have allowed countries to learn from each other's successes and challenges, fostering a collective approach towards sustainable development.

The potential benefits of these collaborations are significant. Firstly, energy diversification is a key goal for both BRICS+ and the GCC. By working together, they can explore alternative energy sources, reduce dependence on fossil fuels, and enhance energy security. This diversification not only reduces exposure to external shocks but also contributes to a more sustainable and resilient energy system.

Secondly, the collaborations in energy cooperation can contribute to reducing greenhouse gas emissions and mitigating climate change impacts. Through the joint promotion of renewable energy sources, both BRICS+ and the GCC actively contribute to the global efforts to combat climate change. This has positive implications for the long-term sustainability of their economies and the well-being of their populations.

Then, the collaborations between BRICS+ and the GCC in the energy field are extensive and promising. These joint efforts have the potential to revolutionise the energy landscape, promote sustainable development, and address pressing environmental challenges. By leveraging their complementary strengths and sharing knowledge and resources, BRICS+ and the GCC are working towards a future where clean and renewable energy sources play a central role in meeting the energy demands of their growing economies. The collaborations between these regions strengthen their energy sectors and demonstrate their commitment to global sustainability goals, showing the world that significant progress can be made in addressing one of the most pressing challenges of our time through cooperation and shared expertise.

The alliances formed between BRICS+ countries, encompassing Brazil, Russia, India, China, South Africa, and other emerging economies, alongside the Gulf Cooperation Council (GCC) countries with notable partners like Saudi Arabia, the United Arab Emirates, Qatar, Kuwait, Oman, and Bahrain, have the potential to shape energy cooperation and spearhead sustainable development initiatives. This extended chapter explores the opportunities, challenges, and strategies for collaboration in the energy sector.

Renewable energy emerges as a central aspect of potential collaboration. The BRICS+ and GCC countries have been investing significantly in renewable energy technologies, including solar, wind, and hydroelectric power. These nations possess vast solar potential, with regions like India's Rajasthan, China's Gansu province, and Saudi Arabia's desert landscapes providing ample opportunities for solar power generation. By sharing their experiences, knowledge, and best practices, the BRICS+ and GCC countries can accelerate the transition towards a low-carbon economy. Collaborative research and development efforts could lead to advancements in renewable energy technologies, improving efficiency and reducing costs. Additionally, deploying renewable energy infrastructure, such as large-scale solar and wind farms, can create new avenues for trade and investment between these countries, facilitating technology transfer and stimulating economic growth.

Another area of focus for energy cooperation lies in infrastructure development. The BRICS+ countries have been actively involved in constructing pipelines, ports, and power grids, while the GCC countries have made substantial investments in mega-infrastructure projects, such as transport networks and smart cities. By aligning their efforts, these regions can enhance energy connectivity and ensure efficient transportation of energy resources. This collaboration could encompass the creation of transnational energy corridors, enabling the seamless energy transfer between the BRICS+ and GCC countries. In doing so, they would strengthen bilateral ties and establish strategic access to energy markets in other regions, contributing to global energy security.

Furthermore, sustainable development initiatives provide a shared objective for the BRICS+ and GCC countries. Recognising the importance of sustainable development in achieving long-term economic growth, alleviating poverty, and preserving the environment, they can work together to promote sustainable practices in the energy sector. This can be achieved through the implementation of energy efficiency measures, the adoption of green technologies, and the exploration of sustainable energy alternatives. Sharing experiences and collaborating on policy frameworks can accelerate the transition to sustainable energy systems, reducing greenhouse gas emissions and mitigating climate change impacts. Furthermore, the BRICS+ and GCC countries can collaborate on sustainable land use practices, water resource management, and conservation efforts to protect their natural environments.

While the potential for energy cooperation and sustainable development initiatives between the BRICS+ and GCC countries is vast, several challenges must be addressed. Diverse energy policies, regulatory frameworks, and market structures can pose hurdles to collaboration. Moreover, geopolitical considerations and diverging national priorities may require careful navigation. To overcome these challenges, open and transparent dialogue platforms must be established. Formal mechanisms, such as joint working groups, high-level forums, and regular conferences, can facilitate knowledge sharing, foster understanding, and identify areas of mutual interest. These platforms must strive to create an inclusive environment for all stakeholders, including governments, industry leaders, academia, and civil society, to steer energy cooperation and sustainable development efforts collectively.

Promoting investment and technology transfer is also crucial to realising the full potential of collaboration between the BRICS+ and GCC countries. Facilitating investment frameworks, incentives, and joint ventures can attract financing for renewable energy projects and infrastructure development. Encouraging research and development partnerships can spur innovation in energy technologies and reduce costs. Additionally, effective mechanisms for technology transfer, including capacity-building programmes and platforms for sharing intellectual property rights, are needed to foster the widespread adoption of sustainable energy solutions. Financial institutions and international organisations can provide funding, technical assistance, and risk mitigation tools to support these collaborative endeavours.

Finally, fostering people-to-people exchanges and cultural diplomacy between the BRICS+ and GCC countries can deepen bonds and promote long-term collaboration. The two regions can leverage their expertise and pool resources to address common challenges in the energy sector by facilitating academic collaborations, research partnerships, and educational exchanges. Scholarships and mobility programmes can enable students, researchers, and professionals to gain exposure to diverse energy systems, policies, and practices. Cultural exchanges, like festivals and exhibitions, allow for greater understanding and appreciation of each other's traditions, values, and aspirations. These people-centred interactions will create a solid foundation for sustainable energy collaboration, nurturing a network of experts and advocates to drive the collective effort towards a sustainable and prosperous future.

In conclusion, energy cooperation and sustainable development initiatives hold immense potential for collaboration between the BRICS+ and GCC countries. These regions can actively contribute to global energy security and sustainability by leveraging their energy resources, knowledge, and expertise. Overcoming challenges will require sustained efforts and strategic political, economic, and societal coordination. By engaging in open dialogue, promoting investment and technology transfer, and fostering people-to-people exchanges, the BRICS+ and GCC countries can forge a resilient partnership capable of addressing energy challenges, spearheading sustainable development, and providing a blueprint for a prosperous future.

35

CASE STUDY 2: TECHNOLOGICAL EXCHANGES AND INNOVATION PARTNERSHIPS

— ◆ —

T his case study delves into the exciting realm of technological exchanges and innovation partnerships between the BRICS+ consortium and the Gulf Cooperation Council (GCC). As the world increasingly relies on technology and innovation to drive economic growth and societal development, examining the collaborations in this area becomes crucial. This chapter explores the opportunities, challenges, potential outcomes, and the socio-economic impact of such partnerships.

Scope and Objectives:

The primary objective of this case study is to assess the current state and future potential of technological exchanges and innovation partnerships between BRICS+ and the GCC. We aim to provide insights into the existing frameworks, initiatives, and areas of cooperation, as well as recommend strategies to enhance further and expand these collaborations. By examining successful case studies, we hope to inspire new ideas and approaches for mutually beneficial technological exchanges and understand the comprehensive impact of these partnerships on society.

Examining Existing Frameworks:

A wide range of frameworks facilitates the landscape of technological exchanges and innovation partnerships between BRICS+ and the GCC. Bilateral agreements between individual countries within the BRICS+ and GCC regions form the foundation of cooperation. For instance, the Memorandum of Understanding on Innovation Cooperation between Brazil and Saudi Arabia has led to collaborative projects in various sectors, such as agriculture, energy, and healthcare. Similarly, the BRICS Science, Technology, and Innovation Framework Programme, initiated in 2015, has facilitated research co-operation and joint projects among BRICS countries. This framework has paved the way for exchanging technological know-how in space technology, renewable energy, and advanced computing sectors. At the regional level, multilateral initiatives like the GCC Framework for Scientific and Technological Cooperation provide a platform for member countries to collaborate on research and development initiatives. Such frameworks enable technology transfer, foster innovation, and promote socio-economic development within the BRICS+ and GCC regions.

Identifying Key Areas of Cooperation:

The potential for technological exchanges and innovation partnerships between BRICS+ and the GCC spans various sectors. Information technology, including software de-velopment and data analytics, has emerged as a major area of cooperation due to the rapid digitalisation in both regions. Artificial intelligence (AI) and machine learning have gained significant attention, with collaborative projects focusing on AI-driven solutions for healthcare, finance, and smart cities. China's advanced expertise in AI and India's prowess in software development, for example, are complementary strengths that can fuel innovation and create novel solutions. Clean energy partnerships addressing renewable energy generation, energy efficiency, and sustainable transportation have also gained mo-mentum. Initiatives such as the BRICS Clean Energy Research Centre and joint efforts to develop smart grids and sustainable transportation systems highlight the potential for collaboration in this sector. Biotechnology collaborations aim to cultivate healthcare, agriculture, and biopharmaceutical research breakthroughs. Joint research initiatives in genomics, bioinformatics, and crop improvement have the potential to address common challenges and drive sustainable agricultural practices. Furthermore, manufacturing, ro-botics, and automation advancements have fuelled joint efforts to enhance production capabilities and industrial efficiency. Collaborative projects in these areas can improve productivity and increase competitiveness and job creation while ensuring sustainable growth.

Success Stories and Lessons Learnt:

Several success stories offer valuable insights into the positive impact of technological exchanges and innovation partnerships between BRICS+ and the GCC. One such example is the collaboration between Indian and Saudi Arabian companies to develop AI-driven solutions in healthcare. They created innovative applications for disease diagnosis, telemedicine, and personalised healthcare through joint research and knowledge sharing. The successful implementation of these solutions improved healthcare outcomes in both regions and fostered economic growth and job creation. Similarly, the cooperation between Chinese and Brazilian companies in renewable energy has resulted in cutting-edge solar panel manufacturing and wind energy production technologies. These success stories highlight the importance of building long-term relationships, leveraging complementary strengths, and aligning projects with societal needs. Additionally, sustained government support, conducive regulatory frameworks, and the integration of academia, industry, and research institutions have played crucial roles in the success of these partnerships.

Addressing Challenges and Barriers:

While technological exchanges and innovation partnerships offer immense potential, they also encounter numerous challenges and barriers. Intellectual property rights (IPR) protection is a pervasive concern, as innovations created through collaborations need reliable mechanisms for IPR registration, enforcement, and equitable sharing of benefits. Collaborating parties must establish clear agreements on ownership, licencing, and commercialisation of intellectual property to ensure fairness and transparency. Regulatory frameworks often vary between countries, hindering smooth collaboration and technology transfer. Harmonising regulations, simplifying bureaucratic processes, and establishing mutual recognition of standards can facilitate smoother collaboration and knowledge exchange. Skill gaps and the need for talent development pose challenges, requiring joint efforts to bridge the divide through capacity-building programmes and exchange programmes for researchers and professionals. Collaborative initiatives between educational institutions, industry stakeholders, and government agencies can address these skill gaps and develop a well-trained workforce. Cultural differences and language barriers can also impede effective communication and collaboration, necessitating the establishment of cultural exchange initiatives and language training programmes. Building cultural understanding, fostering open dialogue, and promoting diversity in collaborative teams can enhance cooperation and innovation. Additionally, securing funding and investment for joint projects and mitigating political tensions between countries can be obstacles diplomatic efforts must overcome. Engaging diplomats, industry leaders, and policymakers in strategic dialogues and leveraging international organizations' support can help overcome these barriers.

Recommendations and Strategies:

Several recommendations and strategies can be employed to enhance further technological exchanges and innovation partnerships between BRICS+ and the GCC. Establishing dedicated technology transfer platforms that connect innovators, entrepreneurs, and investors will facilitate a seamless exchange of technology and knowledge. These platforms can act as hubs for showcasing innovative projects, matching potential partners, and providing access to funding opportunities. Building upon existing collaborative efforts, research and development programmes should be promoted to identify common challenges and drive breakthrough innovations. Encouraging entrepreneurship and fostering start-up ecosystems through joint incubation centres, angel investor networks, and cross-border mentoring initiatives will create an environment conducive to innovation and economic growth. Governments and industry stakeholders can collaborate to provide mentorship programmes, access to funding, and regulatory support to nurture start-ups and scale-ups. Furthermore, facilitating knowledge sharing through capacity-building initiatives and joint academic programmes will nurture a pool of skilled professionals capable of driving technological advancements. Collaborative research initiatives, scholarship programmes, and exchange programmes for students and researchers can bridge the skill gap and build a collaborative talent network. Regular policy dialogues and consultations should be conducted to address regulatory harmonisation, IPR protection, and standardisation, ensuring a level playing field for all partners. These dialogues can help streamline collaboration, overcome bureaucratic hurdles, and foster a favourable business environment. Finally, cultural exchange programmes, networking events, and technology showcases can help bridge cultural gaps and foster strong relationships among innovators, researchers, and entrepreneurs. Platforms that unite diverse stakeholders for cultural exchange, knowledge sharing, and networking can facilitate mutual understanding, trust, and collaboration.

Conclusion:

In conclusion, this extended case study comprehensively examines technological exchanges and innovation partnerships between the BRICS+ consortium and the Gulf Cooperation Council. By exploring successful case studies, identifying key areas of cooperation, addressing challenges, and providing recommendations, we have shed light on these collaborations' immense potential and socio-economic impact. The technological advancements resulting from such partnerships not only address global challenges but also drive economic growth, create job opportunities, and improve the quality of life for the people in these regions. The success stories highlighted in this study inspire other countries and regions to forge their own partnerships and leverage technology for innovation and development.

However, it is important to acknowledge that the path to successful technological exchanges and innovation partnerships is not without its challenges. Intellectual property rights, regulatory differences, skill gaps, cultural barriers, and political tensions can all hinder collaboration and knowledge sharing. To overcome these obstacles, a multi-faceted approach is needed.

Firstly, governments and industry stakeholders must work together to establish clear frameworks and agreements for intellectual property rights protection, including ownership, licencing, and fair sharing of benefits. Harmonising regulatory frameworks and streamlining bureaucratic processes will facilitate smoother collaboration and technology transfer. Capacity-building programmes and exchange initiatives should be implemented to bridge skill gaps and foster a well-trained workforce. Cultural exchange programmes and language training can promote cultural understanding and effective communication among collaborators. Diplomatic efforts must be made to mitigate political tensions and secure funding and investments for joint projects.

Additionally, establishing dedicated platforms for technology transfer and innovation will provide a seamless way for innovators, entrepreneurs, and investors to connect and collaborate. These platforms can serve as hubs for showcasing innovative projects, matching potential partners, and providing access to funding opportunities. Encouraging entrepreneurship and fostering start-up ecosystems through incubation centres, investor networks, and mentoring initiatives will create an environment conducive to innovation and economic growth. Collaboration between governments, industry stakeholders, and educational institutions is crucial in providing mentorship programmes, access to funding, and regulatory support for start-ups and scale-ups. Regular policy dialogues and consultations should be conducted to address regulatory harmonisation, IPR protection, and standardisation.

Finally, technological exchanges and innovation partnerships between BRICS+ and the GCC hold immense potential for driving economic growth, fostering innovation, and addressing global challenges. By harnessing the strengths and expertise of each region, collaborative projects in sectors such as information technology, clean energy, biotechnology, and manufacturing can pave the way for sustainable development. To fully realise the benefits of these partnerships, governments, industry stakeholders, and educational institutions must work together to overcome challenges, foster an enabling environment for innovation, and establish mechanisms for technology transfer and knowledge sharing. This study's case studies and recommendations serve as a roadmap for realising the full potential of technological exchanges and innovation partnerships between BRICS+ and the GCC.

36

CASE STUDY 3: CULTURAL DIPLOMACY AND PEOPLE-TO-PEOPLE EXCHANGES

— • —

This chapter will explore the case study of cultural diplomacy and people-to-people exchanges between the BRICS+ consortium and the Gulf Cooperation Council (GCC) in greater detail. Cultural diplomacy, which is a powerful tool in international relations, plays a pivotal role in promoting dialogue, fostering better understanding, and deepening ties between countries. By emphasizing the significance of cultural exchange programs and people-to-people interactions, this extended case study aims to uncover the potential for mutual benefits and enhanced cooperation between BRICS+ and the GCC in the cultural realm.

1. Historical Context:

The historical ties and cultural interactions between BRICS+ and the GCC countries reveal a rich tapestry of shared cultural heritage that has developed over centuries. The Indian Ocean trade routes, which connected Africa, Asia, and the Middle East, facilitated the exchange of goods, ideas, and cultural practices. The influence of Arab traders on India, the spread of Indian influence in Southeast Asia, and the historical interactions between sub-Saharan Africa and the Arabian Peninsula are all examples of the deep-rooted connections that exist between these regions.

The era of colonialism also significantly shaped the cultural dynamics between BRICS+ and the GCC countries. The presence of Portuguese, Dutch, and British colonial powers in India, South Africa, and parts of the Gulf, respectively, resulted in a cross-pollination of cultural practices, languages, and traditions. These historical legacies continue to shape the cultural landscape and provide a foundation for cultural diplomacy initiatives.

2. Cultural Diplomacy Strategies:

BRICS+ and the GCC countries employ various strategies to enhance their soft power through cultural diplomacy. Cultural exchange programmes, such as youth exchange programmes, artist residencies, and cultural showcases, aim to foster understanding, appreciation, and respect for different cultures. These initiatives provide platforms for artists, scholars, and creative thinkers to collaborate and share their diverse perspectives, promoting dialogue and empathy.

Cultural festivals and exhibitions catalyse cultural diplomacy by celebrating each region's unique heritage and artistic expression. They not only attract international visitors but also facilitate intercultural communication and collaboration. The prominent role of cultural ambassadors, who serve as cultural bridges between BRICS+ and the GCC countries, reinforces the importance of individuals in shaping the perception and understanding of their respective cultures.

3. Educational and Scholarly Exchanges:

Educational and scholarly exchanges cultivate mutual understanding and foster cultural enrichment between BRICS+ and the GCC countries. Student exchange programmes allow students to experience different cultures firsthand, improving cross-cultural communication and building lasting connections.

Joint research projects and academic collaborations provide opportunities for scholars to exchange knowledge and expertise, contributing to the advancement of various academic fields. These collaborations also contribute to a deeper appreciation for cultural diversity and encourage innovative problem-solving by integrating diverse perspectives.

4. Cultural Heritage Preservation and Tourism:

Preserving and promoting cultural heritage sites and landmarks within BRICS+ and GCC countries contribute significantly to cultural diplomacy efforts. By protecting and showcasing their cultural heritage, nations can forge stronger identities, preserve historical narratives, and attract tourists interested in experiencing authentic cultural experiences.

Cultural tourism is crucial in fostering economic growth and strengthening cultural understanding. It offers tourists the opportunity to engage with local communities, participate in cultural activities, and gain insights into the host country's traditions, history, and values. Sustainable tourism practices prioritising the preservation of local cultural traditions and environmental conservation contribute to the long-term sustainability of cultural heritage and tourism initiatives.

5. Language and Intercultural Communication:

Language learning initiatives, translation projects, and intercultural communication efforts are essential in bridging cultural divides and fostering effective communication between BRICS+ and the GCC countries. By promoting language proficiency in each other's languages, nations can overcome language barriers and facilitate better intercultural understanding.

The use of technology and digital platforms to promote language learning and intercultural communication has become increasingly prevalent in recent years. Online language courses, language exchange programmes, and virtual cultural exchanges allow individuals to connect and learn from each other despite geographical distances. These technological advancements provide new avenues for fostering cross-cultural understanding and global dialogue.

6. Challenges and Opportunities:

While cultural diplomacy presents immense opportunities, it also faces challenges that must be addressed for successful outcomes. Cultural differences, varying political contexts, and historical grievances can pose barriers to effective cultural diplomacy efforts. Navigating these challenges requires open dialogue, sensitivity, and multilateral cooperation.

However, these obstacles also present opportunities for creative solutions. Investing in cultural education, leveraging digital platforms, and prioritising long-term partnerships can help overcome challenges and deepen cultural understanding. By embracing cultural diversity and engaging in meaningful cultural exchanges, BRICS+ and the GCC countries can chart a path towards a more interconnected and harmonious future.

7. Lessons Learnt and Best Practices:

Learning from successful cultural diplomacy initiatives and people-to-people exchanges between BRICS+ and the GCC countries provides valuable insights for other regions and nations seeking to strengthen global relations through culture. Sharing best practices and success stories empowers governments, organisations, and individuals to design and implement effective cultural exchange programmes.

Policies that recognise the importance of cultural diplomacy allocate resources for cultural initiatives, and encourage grassroots participation can lead to long-term positive outcomes. Building trust, promoting diversity, and ensuring equal representation are critical factors for successful cultural diplomacy. Cultural diplomacy can build a sustainable foundation for global peace and cooperation by fostering genuine intercultural understanding.

By delving further into this extensive case study on cultural diplomacy and people-to-people exchanges, we understand the potential for cultural collaboration between BRICS+ and the GCC. This extended exploration reinforces the immense transformative power of cultural exchanges in building bridges between nations, fostering appreciation for diverse cultures, and shaping a more harmonious and interconnected global order.

37

CASE STUDY 4: CLIMATE CHANGE MITIGATION AND ADAPTATION STRATEGIES

— ◇ —

C limate change is one of the most pressing challenges facing our world today, and it requires collective efforts from countries and regions to mitigate its impacts and adapt to the changes already in motion. This case study delves deeper into the collaborations between the BRICS+ consortium and the Gulf Cooperation Council (GCC) in addressing climate change and developing effective mitigation and adaptation strategies.

Climate change is one of humanity's most pressing challenges in today's world. Countries and regions must collaborate collectively to mitigate the impacts of climate change and adapt to the changes that are already in motion. This case study closely examines collaborations between the BRICS+ consortium and the Gulf Cooperation Council (GCC) in addressing climate change and developing effective strategies for both mitigation and adaptation.

The Importance of Collective Efforts - BRICS+ and GCC in Climate Change

The BRICS+ consortium, composed of Brazil, Russia, India, China, South Africa, and other key countries, recognises the significance of collective action in mitigating and adapting to climate change. This coalition harnesses the power of emerging economies to work towards common goals, sharing experiences, resources, and expertise to tackle this formidable challenge. Their collaborative efforts aim to foster sustainable development, reduce greenhouse gas emissions, and prioritise adopting renewable energy sources. By leveraging their diverse knowledge and capabilities, the BRICS+ consortium actively contributes to international climate initiatives and ensures the representation of developing nations in global climate negotiations.

Similarly, the Gulf Cooperation Council (GCC) states acknowledge that addressing climate change requires joint endeavours. Bahrain, Kuwait, Oman, Qatar, Saudi Arabia, and the United Arab Emirates work together to implement environmentally friendly policies, promote ecological awareness, and establish regional resilience against climate shocks.

Through these united frontiers, both BRICS+ and GCC reinforce the imperative nature of collective action in preserving our planet for future generations.

Collaborative Measures in Mitigation and Adaptation

Within this framework, the BRICS+ consortium has formed strategic partnerships with the Gulf Cooperation Council (GCC), comprised of six Arab states in the Arabian Peninsula. Together, they aim to develop effective mitigation and adaptation strategies. By conducting thorough research and leveraging the expertise of member countries, the BRICS+ consortium and Gulf Cooperation Council (GCC) will focus on implementing robust collaborative measures. Taking into account the unique challenges faced by Arab states in the Arabian Peninsula, the consortium seeks to identify sustainable solutions for both mitigation and adaptation. Pooling resources and knowledge will enable them to develop innovative strategies that address the region's specific needs while contributing to global efforts to combat climate change.

Through this collaborative endeavour, the BRICS+ consortium and Gulf Cooperation Council (GCC) will prioritise implementing comprehensive measures. Recognising the diverse environmental concerns faced by Arab states in the Arabian Peninsula, the consortium aims to pinpoint lasting solutions for both mitigating and adapting to climate change. By consolidating their collective resources and expertise, they can devise groundbreaking strategies tailored to the region's unique requirements. Through these efforts, these collective organisations will address pressing local challenges and aid global initiatives in combating the worldwide climate crisis.

The ecological landscape in the Arabian Peninsula demands careful attention, as it faces specific challenges such as rapidly increasing temperatures, rising sea levels, frequent sandstorms, and water scarcity. The BRICS+ and Gulf Cooperation Council will coordinate in-depth studies and research ventures to understand the intricacies of these issues thoroughly. They will systematically compile data and assess the impact of climate change on various sectors, including agriculture, energy, water resources, and public health. This concerted effort will provide policymakers and decision-makers valuable insights for formulating evidence-based policies and guidelines.

Moreover, the consortium will facilitate regular exchanges of expertise and experience-sharing between member countries. This knowledge transfer will promote capacity building and enhance the implementation of sustainable practices at both the national and regional levels. Developing countries within the consortium will particularly benefit from this collaboration, gaining access to technology, funding, and expertise from their more developed counterparts. Working collectively will help accelerate progress towards meeting the Sustainable Development Goals set forth by the United Nations, with a specific focus on climate action.

To ensure the success and longevity of these efforts, the BRICS+ consortium and Gulf Cooperation Council will establish a task force dedicated to coordinating and monitoring the implementation of their collaborative initiatives. This task force, comprising experts from relevant fields, will facilitate a steady flow of communication, identify key priority areas, evaluate progress, and propose corrective measures when necessary.

The collaboration between the BRICS+ and GCC further emphasises these member countries' longstanding commitment and dedication to creating a sustainable and resilient future. By leveraging each nation's strengths and acknowledging their geographical disparities, this partnership will drive forward an inclusive and impactful approach to combating climate change. Through robust initiatives, the consortium is set to play an essential role in catalysing global action and shaping a greener, more sustainable world for future generations.

Mitigation Strategies: A Shift Towards Sustainability

Mitigation strategies involve reducing greenhouse gas emissions and promoting sustainable practices. The BRICS+-GCC collaboration emphasises implementing renewable energy projects like solar, wind, and hydroelectric power. By investing in clean energy, these nations are working towards the ambitious targets set in the Paris Agreement.

The efforts to transition to renewable energy have yielded significant results. Adopting solar panels, wind turbines, and hydroelectric power generation has propelled the BRICS countries and GCC nations towards a sustainable future. Their joint commitment to clean energy aligns with the goals outlined in the Paris Agreement. Emphasis is placed on reducing greenhouse gas emissions and promoting a greener approach to energy production. These countries are making substantial strides towards achieving the targets set to combat climate change through collaboration and investment.

The BRICS and GCC nations have accelerated their transition towards a sustainable future through technological advancements and policy initiatives. These nations have shown great commitment to implementing mitigation strategies to reduce greenhouse gas emissions. They have endeavoured to diversify their energy sources with significant investments in solar, wind, and hydroelectric power. This shift towards renewable energy aligns perfectly with the goals established under the Paris Agreement, aiming to combat climate change. By fostering collaboration and sustainable investments, the BRICS and GCC are reshaping their energy landscapes for a greener tomorrow.

Promoting Clean Technologies and Innovation

A key aspect of effective mitigation measures revolves around promoting clean technologies. The collaborations between the BRICS+ consortium and the GCC serve as an incubator for innovative ideas and solutions. They encourage research and development in carbon capture and storage, advanced waste management systems, and sustainable transportation.

These advancements aim to address our planet's pressing environmental concerns. By supporting clean technologies, it paves the way for a sustainable future. The BRICS+ consortium and the GCC foster an environment where forward-thinking solutions flourish. Highlighting the importance of research and development, they prioritise carbon capture and storage advancements, innovative waste management systems, and sustainable transportation. Through this collaboration, they remain relentless in their pursuit of creating a world where innovative technologies play a pivotal role in mitigating climate change.

Through this collaboration, they remain relentless in their pursuit of creating a world where innovative technologies play a pivotal role in mitigating climate change. This monumental effort is backed by dedicated funding from both public and private sectors that resonates with the urgency of the environmental challenges we face. By directing investment towards research and development, the BRICS+ consortium and the GCC strengthen their commitment to fostering sustainable solutions. They envision a future where the interplay between scientific breakthroughs and technological advancements leads us towards a greener and more prosperous world for future generations. Together, they strive to shape the trajectory of clean technologies and innovation and pioneer a sustainable path forward.

Building Resilience through Adaptation Strategies

Adaptation to climate change is equally important in mitigating its impacts. The collaborations between the BRICS+ consortium and the GCC focus on developing adaptive policies and strategies. One prominent area of cooperation involves water resource management and conservation, given the arid climates present within the Gulf countries. They aim to secure water supplies and reduce vulnerabilities through advanced techniques like desalination and efficient irrigation.

This collaboration seeks to serve as a blueprint for other regions facing similar challenges. Alongside water resource management, the consortium has also prioritised efforts in crop diversification to enhance food security. Introducing resilient and drought-tolerant crops aims to minimise the vulnerability caused by water scarcity and changing precipitation patterns. Furthermore, research endeavours targeting coastal areas intend to combat the rising sea levels. Adopting innovative engineering designs can effectively bolster coastal defences and safeguard critical infrastructure. The BRICS+ consortium and the GCC remain committed to adaptive strategies that can successfully address the impacts of climate change.

These adaptive strategies pave the way for a resilient future. Besides water resource management and crop diversification, the collaboration addresses coastal areas' challenges. Their research endeavours aim to counter the escalating sea levels through innovative engineering designs. Implementing these measures can safeguard critical infrastructure against the destructive forces of climate change. The BRICS+ consortium and the GCC strive to create a blueprint for regions grappling with similar issues, emphasising the importance of adaptive policies. Together, they remain dedicated to combatting climate change and its far-reaching impacts.

38

RECOMMENDATIONS AND STRATEGIES

— • —

As the interconnectivity and interdependence between countries continue to grow in the increasingly globalised world, BRICS+ and the Gulf Cooperation Council must strengthen their cooperation and explore avenues for deeper collaboration in various domains. This extended chapter provides a comprehensive and detailed overview of policy recommendations and strategies to enhance economic and trade relations, promote security and regional stability, and advocate for multilateralism and global governance reforms.

One of the key priorities for BRICS+ and the Gulf Cooperation Council is establishing a joint platform for economic collaboration. This platform would be a forum for sharing best practices, identifying synergies, and exploring opportunities for increased investment and trade between the two regions. Regular dialogue and cooperation would allow for the exchange of information on market trends, economic policies, and investment opportunities, facilitating stronger economic ties.

Both regions should focus on diversifying their trade and investment portfolios to promote economic collaboration. This can be achieved through initiatives such as joint investment promotion campaigns, participation in trade exhibitions and fairs, and the establishment of business networking platforms. Encouraging sector-specific collaboration, such as energy cooperation in renewable sources and technology transfer in advanced manufacturing, can open new avenues for trade and investment.

In addition to establishing a joint platform, closer financial cooperation between BRICS+ and the Gulf countries is essential. This can be achieved through strategic partnerships, such as currency swap arrangements or the creation of a BRICS+ and Gulf Development Bank. These initiatives can promote financial stability, facilitate cross-border investments, support infrastructure development, and provide an alternative to the existing global financial architecture.

Furthermore, promoting technological exchanges and innovation partnerships is crucial for the future development of both regions. Collaborations in research and development, technology transfer, and innovation can unlock new opportunities and address common challenges. By sharing knowledge and expertise, both BRICS+ and the Gulf Cooperation Council can harness the power of innovation to drive economic growth, enhance productivity, and foster sustainable development.

Collaboration in security and defence is another vital aspect of BRICS+ and the Gulf Cooperation Council's cooperation. Enhanced security cooperation, such as information-sharing, joint military exercises, and counterterrorism efforts, can contribute to greater stability and security in their respective regions and beyond. By building trust and enhancing joint capabilities, both regions can effectively address security challenges and promote peace in their regions.

To strengthen security cooperation, it is crucial to establish mechanisms for intelligence-sharing and coordination. This can include exchanging information on emerging threats, joint assessments of security risks, and cooperation in cybersecurity. Joint maritime patrols and exercises can also enhance the security of sea lanes and combat piracy and other maritime crimes.

The BRICS+ and Gulf Cooperation Council collaboration should also prioritise sustainable development and environmental protection. Given the global climate crisis and the need to transition to sustainable practices, both regions should share best practices in renewable energy, promote green technologies, and implement policies that mitigate climate change and preserve natural resources. This collaboration can contribute to achieving the Sustainable Development Goals and ensure a more sustainable future for both regions.

Advocating for multilateralism and global governance reforms is essential for BRICS+ and the Gulf countries to exert their influence and shape the future global agenda. Collaborative efforts should focus on advancing reforms to global governance institutions and promoting a rules-based international order. By fostering a more inclusive and equitable global order, both regions can better represent their interests and contribute to addressing global challenges.

Several measures should be adopted to strengthen further economic and trade relations between BRICS+ and the Gulf Cooperation Council. Simplifying trade procedures, reducing trade barriers, and harmonising regulations can create a more conducive environment for businesses in both regions. Exploring the possibility of negotiating free trade agreements and providing preferential access to each other's markets can stimulate economic growth and diversification.

Moreover, promoting sector-specific collaboration is crucial. By identifying sectors of mutual interest, such as energy, technology, agriculture, tourism, and manufacturing, and facilitating collaboration through joint ventures, technology transfers, and knowledge-sharing, both regions can boost innovation, enhance productivity, and create new avenues for economic cooperation.

Regarding security and regional stability, it is essential to strengthen intelligence-sharing and coordination. Establishing mechanisms for sharing intelligence and information can significantly enhance security cooperation and counter potential threats. Active collaboration in counterterrorism efforts, such as sharing best practices in intelligence gathering, border control, and counter-radicalisation strategies, can further contribute to regional stability and security.

Collaboration in addressing regional security challenges, such as conflicts, territorial disputes, and non-proliferation issues, should be fostered through engagement in regular dialogue and consultations. Both regions can contribute to regional stability and peace by promoting confidence-building measures and diplomatic engagements. Additionally, enhancing maritime security cooperation through joint patrols, information-sharing mechanisms, and capacity-building initiatives can effectively combat piracy and transnational organised crime and ensure freedom of navigation in various maritime domains.

In advocating for multilateralism and global governance reforms, BRICS+ and the Gulf countries should actively engage in international forums such as the United Nations, supporting reforms that enhance the representation of emerging economies. Strengthening regional and international institutions is another crucial aspect of this advocacy, focusing on making them more representative, inclusive, and effective in addressing global challenges. Promoting South-South cooperation by enhancing partnerships with other emerging economies and developing countries should also be encouraged to support sustainable development and inclusive growth.

39

Policy Recommendations for BRICS+ and Gulf Cooperation Council

— • —

1. Enhancing Economic Cooperation and Trade Relations

As BRICS+ and Gulf Cooperation Council (GCC) countries aim to strengthen economic ties, prioritising enhancing trade relations is crucial. This can be achieved by promoting the facilitation of trade and investment through the reduction of non-tariff barriers and simplification of customs procedures. Implementing efficient trade facilitation measures, such as single-window systems and harmonised customs regulations, can significantly improve the ease of doing business and attract more foreign investments.

In addition, establishing free trade agreements or preferential trade arrangements among BRICS+ and GCC member countries would further enhance market access and foster economic integration. Such agreements could go beyond the traditional focus on goods, including services, investments, intellectual property rights, and government procurement. By expanding the coverage of trade agreements, countries can tap into new sectors with high growth potential, such as digital services, e-commerce, and the knowledge-based economy.

Furthermore, to ensure the sustainability and stability of economic cooperation, BRICS+ and GCC countries should strengthen financial integration. This can be achieved by increasing cooperation in monetary and exchange rate policies, promoting stability, and reducing volatility in the global economy. Closer coordination between central banks and regulatory authorities will facilitate the development of efficient payment and settlement systems, enabling faster and more secure cross-border transactions.

Exploring establishing regional payment systems or settlement mechanisms would further enhance financial connectivity and reduce reliance on the dominant global financial centres.

2. Promoting Technology and Innovation Partnerships

The rapid advancement of technology and the increasing importance of innovation have significant implications for economic growth and competitiveness. BRICS+ and GCC countries should foster collaboration in research and development, innovation, and technology transfer to promote knowledge-sharing and mutually beneficial outcomes.

Establishing joint research centres and collaborative networks can facilitate the exchange of scientific expertise and promote breakthroughs in key areas. By leveraging each country's strengths and resources, BRICS+ and GCC countries can collectively address complex global challenges, such as climate change, healthcare, and food security.

To foster a culture of innovation and entrepreneurship, joint initiatives should be launched to support startups, incubators, and accelerators across the regions. Access to funding, mentoring, and infrastructure is crucial for nurturing a vibrant startup ecosystem. Joint financing mechanisms, such as venture capital funds, can provide the necessary resources and expertise to turn innovative ideas into successful businesses.

Additionally, establishing joint technology parks and innovation hubs will create an enabling environment for collaboration, knowledge exchange, and commercialisation. By clustering research institutions, startups, and industry players in these hubs, BRICS+ and GCC countries can create ecosystems that fuel innovation and attract investments. These hubs should prioritise emerging technologies such as artificial intelligence, renewable energy, health sciences, and biotechnology, as they offer substantial opportunities for economic diversification and sustainable development.

3. Boosting Infrastructure Development and Connectivity:

Infrastructure development fosters economic growth, facilitates trade, and enhances regional connectivity. BRICS+ and GCC countries should actively pursue investment and cooperation in infrastructure projects to unlock their full potential.

Investments in transportation infrastructure, including ports, airports, railways, and highways, are imperative to improve logistics efficiencies and reduce transportation costs. Joint efforts to address bottlenecks and invest in infrastructure corridors connecting the regions will facilitate the movement of goods and services. Additionally, investment in digital infrastructure, including broadband connectivity and data centres, is essential for bridging the digital divide and promoting digital economies.

BRICS+ and GCC countries should engage national and multilateral development banks to finance infrastructure projects. These institutions can provide funding, technical expertise, and risk mitigation instruments to support sustainable and inclusive infrastructure development. Exploring innovative financing mechanisms, such as public-private partnerships, green bonds, and sovereign wealth fund investments, can further enhance the availability of capital for infrastructure projects.

To maximise infrastructure development benefits, efforts should be made to ensure social inclusiveness and environmental sustainability. Infrastructure projects should adhere to strict environmental standards, consider local communities' needs, and promote employment opportunities. Robust governance frameworks, transparency, and effective project management mechanisms are essential to mitigate risks and ensure the successful implementation of infrastructure projects.

4. Strengthening Security Cooperation and Regional Stability:

Promoting security cooperation and maintaining regional stability are crucial for the long-term prosperity of BRICS+ and GCC countries. Threats such as terrorism, extremism, and cybercrime require concerted efforts and enhanced intelligence-sharing mechanisms to combat them effectively.

BRICS+ and GCC countries should establish intelligence-sharing mechanisms to exchange timely and reliable information on potential security threats. Intelligence agencies should deepen their collaboration and establish joint task forces focused on counterterrorism efforts. Increased sharing of intelligence and best practices will enable a more proactive approach to identifying and neutralising security risks.

Joint military exercises, training programmes, and exchanges among armed forces will enhance interoperability and build capacity to address regional security challenges effectively. Cooperation in maritime security, border control, and cybersecurity is particularly critical as these areas directly impact regional stability. Regular dialogues at the defence and security levels among BRICS+ and GCC countries will foster mutual trust and understanding, paving the way for greater synergy in tackling shared security challenges.

To strengthen conflict resolution and crisis management efforts, BRICS+ and GCC countries should initiate dialogue platforms to promote peaceful resolutions to regional conflicts. These platforms should facilitate open and constructive conversations, encouraging sharing of experiences and perspectives. By working collectively, BRICS+ and GCC countries can contribute to conflict prevention, peacebuilding, and regional stability.

5. Promoting Sustainable Development and Climate Change Mitigation:

Sustainability has become a paramount concern for the global community. BRICS+ and GCC countries should prioritise sustainable development and climate change mitigation as integral to their policy agendas.

Collaborative efforts are needed to address climate change by promoting renewable energy deployment, energy efficiency, and conservation measures. Sharing experiences, best practices, and research findings on renewable energy technologies can accelerate the transition toward a low-carbon economy. Given both regions' abundance of solar and wind energy resources, joint initiatives should be explored to promote renewable energy generation, including establishing renewable energy centres of excellence.

Efficient and sustainable water resource management is another crucial aspect of sustainable development. BRICS+ and GCC countries can share expertise in desalination technologies, irrigation methods, and water conservation measures. Collaborative initiatives for water management, such as joint research projects, capacity-building programmes, and knowledge-sharing platforms, can help address water scarcity concerns and ensure water security for all.

Furthermore, BRICS+ and GCC countries should support initiatives and funding mechanisms for green finance and sustainable investment. Encouraging and facilitating investments in sustainable projects, renewable energy, and clean technologies can drive sustainable economic growth and align regional development goals with global sustainability objectives. Exploring green bonds, impact investments, and sustainability-linked investment incentives will attract capital flows to environmentally sound projects.

To effectively address sustainable development challenges, exchanging ideas and experiences on environmental management, conservation of natural resources, and sustainable land use is essential. Platforms for regular dialogue and information sharing, such as workshops, conferences, and research networks, should be established to facilitate the dissemination of knowledge and the adoption of best practices.

6. Advocating for Multilateralism and Global Governance Reforms:

BRICS+ and GCC countries have a significant role in advocating for multilateralism, reinforcing the importance of global governance reforms, and strengthening the rules-based order. These countries should actively engage in global forums, such as the United Nations, G20, World Trade Organisation (WTO), and International Monetary Fund (IMF), to advocate for a more inclusive, fair, and effective global governance system.

BRICS+ and GCC countries should collectively push for reforms in international institutions to better reflect the changed global dynamics and ensure the participation of all countries in decision-making processes. This includes efforts to increase the representation and voice of developing countries in global institutions, particularly in the IMF and World Bank. Reforms should also aim to enhance the effectiveness and efficiency of these institutions in addressing global challenges, such as financial stability, poverty eradication, and sustainable development.

Furthermore, BRICS+ and GCC countries should firmly support multilateralism and advocate for a rules-based international order. By upholding the principles of mutual respect, dialogue, and cooperation, these countries can counterbalance unilateralism, protectionism, and any attempt to undermine the global trading system. Strengthening regional organisations, such as the BRICS New Development Bank and the GCC, can promote multilateralism and regional cooperation.

Additionally, BRICS+ and GCC countries should promote dialogue and cooperation among diverse cultures, religions, and civilisations. Interfaith dialogues, cultural exchanges, and people-to-people contacts can foster understanding, tolerance, and mutual respect, promoting peace, stability, and social cohesion.

7. Enhancing Human Capital Development and Education Cooperation:

Investing in human capital development is essential for sustainable economic growth and social progress. BRICS+ and GCC countries should prioritise education, skills development, and capacity building to equip their populations with the necessary knowledge and skills for the future.

Cooperation in education should focus on sharing best practices, exchanging students and scholars, and developing joint research programmes. Scholarships and exchange programmes for students and academics can facilitate cultural exchange, knowledge transfer, and the creation of a global talent pool. Joint research projects and collaborative academic initiatives can address common challenges, promote innovation, and contribute to scientific advancements.

In addition to formal education, vocational training and lifelong learning programmes should be promoted to address skills gaps and enhance employability. Joint initiatives for skills development can include training programmes, industry-academia collaboration, and certification schemes. This will help meet the evolving demands of the labour market and foster entrepreneurship and innovation.

Furthermore, BRICS+ and GCC countries should collaborate in developing and deploying digital technologies for education. This includes leveraging e-learning platforms, digital content, and virtual classrooms to ensure equitable access to quality education, particularly in remote and underserved areas. Sharing experiences and best practices in education technology can enhance the effectiveness of digital learning and promote inclusive education.

Conclusion:

BRICS+ and GCC countries have significant potential for enhanced cooperation and mutually beneficial partnerships. By prioritising economic cooperation, technology and innovation, infrastructure development and connectivity, security cooperation, sustainable development, and global governance reforms, these countries can unlock new opportunities, address common challenges, and contribute to global prosperity.

Strong political commitment, effective institutional frameworks, and active stakeholder engagement are crucial for successfully implementing these policy recommendations. Regular dialogue, information sharing, and monitoring mechanisms should be established to ensure effective coordination and progress tracking.

By embracing these recommendations, BRICS+ and GCC countries can strengthen regional integration, contribute to global governance reforms, and foster inclusive and sustainable development in their respective regions and beyond.

40

STRENGTHENING ECONOMIC AND TRADE RELATIONS BETWEEN **BRICS**+ AND **GCC**

— ◆ —

Within the evolving global order context, the economic and trade relations between the BRICS+ consortium and the Gulf Cooperation Council (GCC) countries hold significant potential for growth, cooperation, and mutual benefits. This chapter aims to provide an in-depth analysis and explore strategies to strengthen these relations further, focusing on the economic aspects.

1. Historical Overview:

The economic relations between BRICS+ and GCC countries have witnessed steady growth. The two sides have historically engaged in energy trade, with GCC countries as major oil and gas suppliers to the BRICS+ economies. However, recent years have seen diversification in trade, with increasing engagement in sectors such as manufacturing, agriculture, services, and tourism.

Key milestones and developments include establishing the BRICS+ partnership in 2009, which paved the way for enhanced economic cooperation. In 2018, the BRICS+ cooperation framework expanded to include countries such as Thailand, Indonesia, and Turkey, further strengthening the potential for trade expansion.

2. Opportunities for Trade Expansion:

BRICS+ and GCC countries have significant untapped potential for trade expansion in various sectors. Energy cooperation remains a vital component, with the GCC's rich oil and natural gas resources meeting the energy demands of the BRICS+ economies. However, both sides should look beyond energy and focus on diversifying their trade portfolios. Opportunities lie in sectors such as infrastructure development, information technology, healthcare, education, renewable energy, e-commerce, and tourism.

In infrastructure development, the BRICS+ countries possess advanced expertise and experience in constructing large-scale projects, while the GCC countries have made significant advancements in port development, transportation networks, and logistics. Collaborative efforts to develop transportation corridors, logistics hubs, and robust digital connectivity initiatives will enhance connectivity and regional integration, benefiting trade and investment flows.

Furthermore, the rising digital economies of the BRICS+ consortium present opportunities for collaboration in the technology and innovation sectors. Sharing technological advancements, promoting research and development, and fostering joint initiatives in emerging technologies like artificial intelligence, blockchain, and 5G can contribute to economic diversification and productivity gains.

3. Trade Facilitation and Liberalisation:

To harness the full potential of economic cooperation, streamlining trade facilitation measures and ensuring liberalisation is crucial. Efforts should be made to harmonise customs procedures, reduce non-tariff barriers, and simplify trade documentation requirements to create a smoother cross-border trade environment.

Establishing robust institutional frameworks and effective dispute-resolution mechanisms will give businesses the confidence to engage in cross-border trade. Additionally, exploring regional integration initiatives such as a free trade agreement or preferential trade arrangements will create a stable and predictable trading environment, encouraging greater investments and trade volumes.

With the proliferation of e-commerce and digital trade, both BRICS+ and GCC countries should adopt common standards, enhance cybersecurity frameworks, and facilitate cross-border e-commerce activities, making it easier for businesses to participate in online trade.

4. Investment Promotion:

Promoting investment opportunities and facilitating cross-border investment flows is crucial to fully leverage the potential of economic cooperation between BRICS+ and GCC countries. GCC countries are known for their attractive investment climate, while the BRICS+ countries have demonstrated their potential as emerging markets with favourable growth prospects.

Policies to attract foreign direct investment (FDI) should prioritise sectors such as infrastructure, manufacturing, technology, renewable energy, and healthcare. Encouraging joint ventures, facilitating technology transfer, and providing incentives for investors will further incentivise investment flows.

Additionally, establishing investment protection agreements between the BRICS+ and GCC countries can provide legal certainty, safeguard the interests of investors, and stimulate more significant investment.

5. Finance and Banking Cooperation:

Financial institutions are vital in fostering economic cooperation between BRICS+ and GCC countries. Cooperation between development banks, sovereign wealth funds, and commercial banks can facilitate project financing and investment. Developing currency swap agreements would reduce currency risks and encourage more substantial cross-border trade and investment.

Collaborative efforts should focus on enhancing regulatory frameworks to promote financial stability, sharing best practices in risk management, and exploring innovative financial instruments. Establishing joint investment funds and specialised banking institutions can provide financial support for joint projects and ventures.

Furthermore, promoting Islamic finance, an area of expertise for many GCC countries can offer new avenues for financing infrastructure projects and investment in the BRICS+ consortium.

6. Infrastructure Development:

Infrastructure development is pivotal to increasing connectivity and regional integration. BRICS+ countries possess considerable experience and expertise in infrastructure projects, while the GCC countries have demonstrated excellence in various infrastructure sectors such as transportation, telecommunications, and renewable energy.

The two sides should explore opportunities for joint infrastructure projects, such as transportation corridors, logistics hubs, and digital connectivity initiatives. Public-private partnerships can be encouraged to leverage the expertise of both sides and attract private investment. Technology transfer and knowledge sharing in infrastructure planning and implementation should be promoted.

Moreover, endeavours to strengthen connectivity through initiatives like the Belt and Road Initiative and the Asia Infrastructure Investment Bank can provide additional opportunities for collaboration in infrastructure development between BRICS+ and GCC countries.

7. Innovation and Technology Cooperation:

Embracing innovation and technology cooperation can unlock new avenues for economic growth between BRICS+ and GCC countries. Collaboration in research and development, technology transfer, and knowledge exchange can foster joint initiatives and contribute to economic diversification.

Both sides can nurture entrepreneurship, promote startup ecosystems, and facilitate technology transfer by establishing joint innovation centres and technology incubators. Sharing best practices in advancing digital economies, developing smart cities, and leveraging emerging technologies like artificial intelligence, blockchain, and 5G can enhance economic cooperation.

Furthermore, promoting collaboration in science and technology education can strengthen human capital development and create a skilled workforce to support innovation-driven growth.

8. Promoting Small and Medium-Sized Enterprises (SMEs):

Recognising the role of SMEs in economic growth and job creation and promoting their participation in bilateral trade is essential. Business matching platforms, trade fairs, and joint venture initiatives should be encouraged to connect SMEs from BRICS+ and GCC countries.

Capacity-building programmes, training workshops, and knowledge-sharing platforms can enhance the capabilities of SMEs to navigate cross-border trade, regulations, and market dynamics. Moreover, measures to facilitate financing for SMEs, such as credit guarantee schemes and venture capital provisions, can bolster their participation in bilateral trade and investment.

Supporting and empowering SMEs will contribute to their growth, foster inclusive economic development, and reduce income inequalities within the BRICS+ and GCC countries.

9. Addressing Challenges and Risks:

Despite the promising potential for economic cooperation, several challenges and risks must be addressed to ensure sustainable and fruitful relations between BRICS+ and GCC countries. Political instability, trade protectionism, economic volatility, and regulatory barriers can impede progress.

Building trust and confidence through enhanced dialogue and diplomatic efforts is crucial to overcoming geopolitical tensions. Joint efforts should be made to mitigate trade barriers, harmonise regulatory frameworks, and foster a fair and transparent business environment. Additionally, cooperation in risk assessment and management and creating contingency plans can help mitigate economic uncertainties.

Strengthening people-to-people and cultural exchanges, promoting understanding of each other's business and regulatory environments, and building relationships between business communities and entrepreneurs will reduce cultural and communication barriers and enhance cooperation.

10. Sustainable Development and Environmental Cooperation:

Both BRICS+ and GCC countries share a common interest in sustainable development and environmental protection. Collaboration in renewable energy, climate change mitigation, water resource management, and waste management can foster sustainable economic growth.

Joint initiatives can be undertaken to develop renewable energy projects, promote energy efficiency measures, and share best practices in sustainable development. Collaboration in environmental research, technology transfer, and knowledge exchange can contribute to sustainable resource management and environmental conservation.

Furthermore, exploring opportunities for joint projects in green infrastructure, eco-tourism, and sustainable agriculture can provide avenues for economic diversification and promote long-term sustainability.

Conclusion:

Strengthening economic and trade relations between BRICS+ and GCC countries holds immense potential for growth, cooperation, and mutual benefits. By diversifying trade portfolios, streamlining trade facilitation measures, promoting investment, enhancing financial cooperation, fostering infrastructure development, embracing innovation and technology collaboration, and addressing challenges and risks, both sides can unlock new avenues for economic growth and regional integration.

The success of this endeavour will require strong political will, effective institutional frameworks, enhanced dialogue, and sustained efforts to build trust and understanding. By capitalising on existing synergies and exploring new opportunities, the BRICS+ and GCC countries can forge a stronger economic partnership that contributes to the prosperity and stability of the region and beyond.

41

ENHANCING COLLABORATION IN SECURITY, COUNTERTERRORISM, AND REGIONAL STABILITY

— • —

I n an increasingly interconnected and turbulent world, the need for collaboration between the BRICS+ consortium and the Gulf Cooperation Council (GCC) in security, counterterrorism, and regional stability is paramount. Both alliances recognise the criticality of addressing common security challenges and working together to ensure peace, stability, and prosperity within their regions and beyond. This extended chapter delves deeper into various avenues for enhancing collaboration in security and counterterrorism, exploring the multifaceted dimensions of cooperation between BRICS+ and the GCC.

1. Intelligence Sharing and Information Exchange:

Intelligence sharing and information exchange form the cornerstone of effective counterterrorism efforts. Enhancing collaboration in this domain requires establishing secure and robust communication channels to enable seamless information sharing between BRICS+ and the GCC. The exchange of timely, accurate, and actionable intelligence is crucial to detecting, preventing, and responding to potential threats. To achieve this, both alliances should develop standardised protocols and mechanisms for secure information sharing, ensuring the confidentiality of sensitive data while respecting national security concerns and data privacy. A shared platform or mechanism for intelligence fusion and analysis could further optimise collaborative efforts, enabling a comprehensive understanding of emerging security threats and effective cross-border responses.

2. Joint Military Exercises and Training Programmes:

Joint military exercises and training programmes are invaluable opportunities for BRICS+ and the GCC to strengthen cooperation, enhance interoperability, and improve crisis response capabilities. These exercises should be multifaceted, encompassing land, maritime, and aerial domains, and involve realistic scenarios to simulate real-life security challenges. Regular joint exercises allow member states to develop a deeper understanding of each other's military capabilities, refine joint operational procedures, and identify areas for improved coordination. Additionally, these exercises create shared experiences and build trust among military forces, fostering greater cohesion in peacekeeping operations and cross-border crisis management efforts.

3. Border Security Management and Cross-Border Cooperation:

Given the vast and diverse borders within the BRICS+ and GCC regions, effective border security management and cross-border cooperation are essential. Both alliances should prioritise the development of collaborative frameworks that address common challenges such as smuggling, human trafficking, and illicit trade. Joint border patrols, intelligence-driven risk assessments, and technology-sharing for surveillance systems can bolster security measures, enabling early detection and interdiction of criminal activities. Moreover, establishing cross-border cooperation mechanisms with neighbouring countries beyond BRICS+ and the GCC memberships can contribute to comprehensive regional security by effectively addressing non-state actors and transnational organised crime syndicates.

4. Countering Radicalisation and Violent Extremism:

The threat of radicalisation and violent extremism has become increasingly pervasive, necessitating concerted efforts by BRICS+ and the GCC to develop effective counter-measures. Collaboration in this domain should involve knowledge-sharing on successful initiatives, best practices, and lessons learnt in countering radicalisation. Member states can exchange expertise on implementing comprehensive strategies that address the root causes of radicalisation, ranging from socioeconomic disparities and political grievances to ideological manipulation. Sharing experiences on deradicalization programmes, community engagement models, and youth empowerment initiatives can further strengthen efforts to counter the appeal of extremist ideologies. Engaging with civil society organisations, religious leaders, and community stakeholders is crucial for developing targeted and context-specific interventions to prevent and counter radicalisation.

5. Strengthening Intergovernmental Cooperation Frameworks:

To facilitate and enhance collaboration in security and counterterrorism, BRICS+ and the GCC should prioritise the strengthening of intergovernmental cooperation frameworks. This can be achieved through bilateral and multilateral agreements that provide a legal foundation for information sharing, joint operations, and mutual assistance. Regular dialogue and coordination meetings among security agencies, defence ministries, and policymakers are essential to building trust, maintaining a shared understanding of evolving security challenges and fostering long-term cooperation. Establishing standardised legal frameworks, intelligence-sharing protocols, and operational procedures will streamline collaboration efforts, enabling member states to respond swiftly and effectively to emerging threats.

6. Capacity Building and Technological Advancements:

Building the capacity of security forces and law enforcement agencies within BRICS+ and the GCC is crucial for mitigating security challenges effectively. Collaborative capacity-building initiatives should encompass training programmes, knowledge-sharing platforms, and technical assistance to enhance the capabilities of security personnel. Member states can leverage their strengths and resources to develop specialised training modules in counterterrorism operations, cybersecurity, intelligence analysis, and crisis response. Additionally, collaboration in technological advancements, including developing and deploying cutting-edge surveillance technologies, artificial intelligence, and advanced analytical tools, can significantly augment the effectiveness and efficiency of security operations.

In conclusion, enhancing collaboration in security, counterterrorism, and regional stability between the BRICS+ consortium and the Gulf Cooperation Council is imperative to address the evolving security landscape. By focusing on intelligence sharing, joint military exercises, border security management, countering radicalisation, strengthening intergovernmental cooperation frameworks, and capacity building, these alliances can establish a solid foundation for sustained collaboration. Building trust, establishing robust communication channels, and fostering a culture of information sharing and cooperation will be vital as they strive toward enduring regional stability and global peace.

42

Promoting Multilateralism and Global Governance Reforms

— ◆ —

In today's interconnected world, promoting multilateralism and global governance reforms is crucial to address the complex challenges and ensure a more equitable and sustainable future for all nations. As the global order evolves with the rising influence of the BRICS+ consortium and the Gulf Cooperation Council (GCC), it becomes imperative to foster collaborative efforts among countries to tackle emerging global issues effectively.

One key aspect that needs to be addressed is the need to enhance the role and effectiveness of existing global governance institutions. While institutions such as the United Nations (UN), World Trade Organisation (WTO), World Bank, and International Monetary Fund (IMF) have been instrumental in maintaining global stability and promoting economic development, there is growing recognition that they need to be reformed to reflect better the changing global dynamics.

As the primary global governance institution, the United Nations has faced criticism for its slow decision-making processes and lack of representation from emerging economies. Reforms could focus on increasing the power of the General Assembly, where all member states have equal representation, and ensuring that the Security Council, with its power to authorise military actions and impose sanctions, is more representative and inclusive. This would require expanding the number of permanent and non-permanent members to reflect the geopolitical realities of the twenty-first century.

Similarly, the World Trade Organisation, entrusted with promoting free trade and resolving disputes, should consider reforms to make its decision-making processes more transparent, efficient, and accountable. Ensuring that emerging economies have a stronger voice in shaping trade rules and regulations can help address current imbalances.

The World Bank and the International Monetary Fund, tasked with providing financial assistance and promoting economic stability, must also undergo reforms. Particular attention should be paid to the voting power and decision-making processes within these institutions to reflect the economic realities of the world. Giving emerging economies a greater influence would enhance the legitimacy and effectiveness of these global financial institutions.

Furthermore, global governance reforms should focus on strengthening regional cooperation organisations. The BRICS+ consortium, which includes major emerging economies such as Brazil, Russia, India, China, and South Africa, can potentially be a powerful force for reform. These countries can push for greater representation, inclusivity, and effectiveness within global institutions by joining forces and advocating for their shared interests.

The Gulf Cooperation Council, comprising Gulf countries like Saudi Arabia, the United Arab Emirates, and Qatar, also has a crucial role. It can serve as a cornerstone for regional stability and integration, fostering collaboration and dialogue amongst its member nations. By jointly addressing pressing regional issues such as security, economic development, and climate change, the GCC can contribute to larger global governance reforms.

Reforming global governance also necessitates strengthening the principles of multilateralism and upholding international law. In recent years, some nations have seen a concerning rise in geopolitical tensions and unilateral actions. This threatens the effectiveness of multilateralism and erodes the foundations of global governance. It is crucial to emphasise the importance of adherence to international norms and mechanisms to address disputes, promote peaceful resolution, and foster cooperation among nations.

Moreover, global challenges like climate change, pandemics, terrorism, and poverty require collective actions and shared responsibility. These issues do not respect borders and thus necessitate international collaboration. BRICS+ and the GCC can advocate multilateral approaches, mobilise resources, and share best practices to tackle these complex global issues. By leveraging their diverse experiences and expertise, they can reinforce global governance systems and contribute to sustainable development and prosperity.

To foster multilateralism and global governance reforms, policymakers and stakeholders must take certain actions. First and foremost, fostering dialogue and mutual understanding among nations is essential. Initiating and facilitating dialogue forums where countries exchange views, concerns, and aspirations can help build trust and enhance cooperation. This includes enhancing diplomatic and cultural exchanges and promoting people-to-people connections to foster a sense of shared humanity.

Additionally, supporting initiatives for inclusive global governance structures is crucial. This includes promoting fair representation of emerging economies in global institutions and reforming decision-making processes to ensure the voices of all nations are heard. Encouraging democratic principles and accountability within global organisations can help build trust and legitimacy in decision-making.

Investing in capacity-building measures is equally important. Enhancing developing countries' knowledge, skills, and resources can empower them to engage actively in global governance discussions. This can be achieved through training programmes, technology transfers, and financial support.

Furthermore, greater participation of civil society and non-governmental organisations (NGOs) in global decision-making should be encouraged. These actors represent diverse perspectives and can bring innovative ideas and solutions to the table. Their involvement can help ensure a more inclusive and democratic global governance system. Their role in monitoring the implementation of global agreements and holding governments accountable is invaluable.

In conclusion, promoting multilateralism and global governance reforms is paramount in the changing global order shaped by the BRICS+ consortium and the GCC. These emerging powers can contribute to a more stable, prosperous, and sustainable world by working together and advocating for a fair and inclusive international system. They can reform existing global governance institutions through dialogue, inclusive decision-making processes, and collaboration, bridge gaps, and address pressing global challenges. Now, more than ever, promoting multilateralism and strengthening global governance is crucial to shaping a better future for all.

43

CONCLUSION

— • —

In this book, we have explored in depth the rise of the BRICS+ consortium and its intersecting interests with the Gulf Cooperation Council (GCC). Throughout our analysis of their economic perspectives, energy dynamics, geopolitical implications, strategic convergence, and potential collaborations, we have gained a comprehensive understanding of the implications for the global order and the future of the relationship between BRICS+ and the GCC.

One of the key takeaways from our exploration is the significant transformation in global power dynamics triggered by the emergence of the BRICS+ consortium and the increasing influence of Gulf countries. The Western dominance, which has shaped the global order for decades, is being challenged by the rise of these new players. As their economies shift and their influence grows, new models of cooperation and collaboration are gaining traction, presenting the prospect of a more multipolar world order.

Furthermore, the economic potential of the BRICS+ and GCC alliances cannot be overstated. When we examine their combined resources, expanding markets, and increasingly advanced industries, it becomes evident that these regions can drive global economic growth and foster innovation and technological advancements. The consolidation of economic and trade relations between BRICS+ and the GCC holds the key to unlocking the full economic potential of both regions and paving the way for mutually beneficial trade and investment opportunities.

Another crucial aspect we explored is the security intertwining of BRICS+ and the Gulf countries, which has far-reaching implications for regional stability and counterterrorism efforts. By forging partnerships in security cooperation, intelligence sharing, and investments in military capabilities, both BRICS+ and the GCC can enhance their collective security and contribute to a more stable regional landscape. This collaboration can also extend to infrastructure development and connectivity initiatives, facilitating greater economic integration and cooperation.

As we look towards the future, it is clear that BRICS+ and the GCC will continue to play significant roles in shaping the global order. While there may be both converging and diverging interests between these regions, they have a shared understanding of the need for a more equitable and multipolar world order. Consequently, as BRICS+ and the GCC strengthen their alliances, their collective influence will increase, granting them a greater voice in reshaping global governance and decision-making institutions.

In light of these developments, policymakers and global decision-makers must recognise and capitalise on the growing influence of BRICS+ and the GCC. A more inclusive and representative global order can be achieved by actively seeking opportunities for collaboration and partnership with these regions. As the global landscape evolves, fostering dialogue, enhancing multilateralism, and reforming global governance structures will ensure that all stakeholders have a voice in decision-making.

To sum up, the rise of the BRICS+ consortium and the expanding influence of the Gulf Cooperation Council marks a significant shift in the global order. These regions possess the potential to shape economic, energy, security, and geopolitical dynamics while also fostering innovation, sustainability, and collaboration. The ongoing relationship between BRICS+ and the GCC presents opportunities for mutual growth, cooperation, and creating a more balanced and inclusive global order. Navigating these changes successfully and harnessing the potential that emerges from these alliances will require careful consideration and proactive engagement from policymakers and global leaders.

44

KEY FINDINGS AND INSIGHTS FROM THE BOOK

— • —

This book delves into the multifaceted dynamics of the BRICS+ consortium and the Gulf Cooperation Council (GCC), exploring their intersecting interests and implications for the global order. This final chapter summarises the key findings and insights derived from our in-depth analysis.

1. Economic Growth and Development Patterns among BRICS+ Countries:

The BRICS+ countries, encompassing Brazil, Russia, India, China, and others, have emerged as powerful players in the global economy. Our analysis has revealed that these nations have experienced remarkable economic growth and development trajectories over the past few decades. Despite experiencing periodic economic challenges, such as Russia's economic downturn and Brazil's recession, these countries have demonstrated resilience and strong macroeconomic fundamentals. Their combined GDP and trade volumes have risen significantly, challenging the traditional dominance of Western economies. China, in particular, has emerged as a global economic powerhouse, with its rapid industrialisation and large consumer base fuelling its growth. This economic expansion has allowed BRICS+ countries to increase their influence and actively shape global economic and financial policies.

2. Crucial Role of the GCC as Global Energy Suppliers:

The GCC countries, on the other hand, hold immense significance as major global energy suppliers. Rich in oil and natural gas reserves, these nations play a pivotal role in meeting global energy demands. The GCC's combined oil production accounts for a substantial portion of the world's total, allowing it to shape the global energy market and influence prices. The GCC countries act as vital energy suppliers to developed and developing economies with their production capacities and strategic geographic locations. The stability of the GCC's energy market is crucial for maintaining global energy security and stability.

3. Potential for Collaboration between BRICS+ and the GCC:

Despite their geographical and cultural differences, our analysis has unveiled substantial potential for collaboration and partnerships between BRICS+ and the GCC. Recognising the benefits of cooperation, several initiatives and forums have been established to enhance economic ties and promote dialogue between the two groups. One such initiative is the BRICS+GCC Business Forum, which aims to foster economic collaboration by connecting businesses and facilitating trade and investment. Encouraging interactions and exchanges between entrepreneurs, investors, and policymakers from both sides creates opportunities for joint ventures, technology transfers, and knowledge sharing. This collaboration would enhance economic ties and foster cultural exchange, technological advancements, and broader regional stability.

4. Geopolitical Implications:

The rise of BRICS+, along with the growing influence of the GCC, has significant geopolitical implications. The shifting global power dynamics, coupled with the increasing assertiveness of emerging powers, challenge the existing global order and call for a recalibration of international relations. The United States, as a dominant force, faces the challenge of adapting to these evolving power dynamics while reassessing its relationships with emerging powers. As BRICS+ and the GCC assert their influence, there is a need for the United States and other Western powers to navigate this changing landscape and engage in constructive dialogue and cooperation. Failure to do so could lead to increased geopolitical tensions and potential conflicts.

5. Strategic and Economic Convergence:

Through a detailed analysis of existing and potential areas of collaboration, we have identified strategic and economic convergence opportunities between BRICS+ and the GCC. Collaborative efforts encompass security cooperation, counterterrorism initiatives, infrastructure development, and connectivity projects such as the Belt and Road Initiative. The BRICS+ countries can leverage the GCC's expertise in energy production and infrastructure development to bolster their own efforts in sustainable development. Similarly, the GCC can tap into the technological advancements and diverse markets of the BRICS+ nations to diversify their economies and reduce dependence on hydrocarbon exports. Both sides can enhance their capacity to address shared challenges, increase regional stability, and stimulate economic growth by pooling their resources, expertise, and capabilities.

6. Implications for the Global Order:

The rise of BRICS+ and the GCC collectively challenges traditional Western dominance and calls for a more inclusive and multipolar world order. While the United States remains a significant global player, the combined influence of emerging powers cannot be disregarded. Policymakers and global decision-making institutions must recognise the perspectives and interests of BRICS+ and the GCC when formulating policies and shaping the global agenda. Embracing a multipolar approach can lead to more equitable and effective global governance structures. International organisations, such as the United Nations, World Trade Organisation, and International Monetary Fund, must adapt and evolve to accommodate the changing power dynamics and ensure all voices are heard and represented.

7. Case Studies:

The book presented a series of case studies demonstrating the potential for collaboration between BRICS+ and the GCC. These studies focus on diverse areas such as energy cooperation, sustainable development, technological exchanges, innovation partnerships, cultural diplomacy, people-to-people exchanges, and climate change mitigation and adaptation strategies. For instance, the case study on energy cooperation highlights the possibility of joint investments in renewable energy projects, technology transfers, and knowledge sharing to accelerate the transition towards a low-carbon economy. Similarly, the case study on innovation partnerships explores the potential for joint research and development initiatives in fields such as robotics, artificial intelligence, and biotechnology. By examining these exemplars of cooperation, we gain practical insights into the possibilities and tangible benefits that can be realised through enhanced collaboration between BRICS+ and the GCC.

In conclusion, this book has provided comprehensive insights into the rise of the BRICS+ consortium and the Gulf Cooperation Council, exploring their economic perspectives, energy dynamics, intersecting interests, geopolitical implications, strategic and economic convergence, and implications for the global order. The key findings and insights highlighted emphasise the pressing need for enhanced cooperation, collaboration, and mutual understanding between these powerful entities. As the world continues to evolve, the relationships and interactions between BRICS+ and the GCC will undoubtedly play pivotal roles in shaping the future of the global order and influencing the direction of global affairs.

45

THE ONGOING RELATIONSHIP BETWEEN BRICS+ AND THE GULF COOPERATION COUNCIL

— • —

The relationship between the BRICS+ consortium and the Gulf Cooperation Council (GCC) holds significant potential for collaboration and cooperation. Both entities have emerged as major players in the global order, with their economic, geopolitical, and strategic interests intersecting in various ways.

The BRICS+ consortium, comprising Brazil, Russia, India, China, South Africa, and other emerging economies, has driven global economic growth and development. These countries boast some of the world's largest and most dynamic economies, accounting for a substantial global GDP and trade share. Their collective influence on global governance issues has steadily increased, challenging the traditional dominance of Western powers in shaping international policies and regulations.

With its vast natural resources and diverse economy, Brazil is a key player in the consortium. Its agricultural sector is a major global exporter, contributing significantly to global food security. Russia, endowed with vast mineral reserves and advanced technological capabilities, holds a prominent position in energy markets and defence industries. The world's largest democracy, India, is a dynamic market with a growing middle class, a thriving technology sector, and a prominent role in global services outsourcing. China, the world's second-largest economy, has transformed into a global manufacturing hub, shifting from export-oriented growth to domestic consumption-driven expansion. With its mineral wealth, solid financial sector, and vibrant tourism industry, South Africa serves as a gateway to the African continent, attracting investment flows from around the world.

Meanwhile, the Gulf Cooperation Council comprises six energy-rich countries in the Gulf region: Saudi Arabia, United Arab Emirates, Qatar, Kuwait, Bahrain, and Oman.

These nations have accrued immense wealth and power thanks to their vast oil and natural gas reserves. As significant players in the global energy market, they hold substantial economic sway and influence global energy prices. Additionally, their geographic proximity to major trade routes and their strategic location make them vital hubs for global trade and commerce.

Saudi Arabia, considered the de facto leader of the GCC, is the world's largest oil producer and exporter. Its Vision 2030 economic reform plan aims to diversify the Saudi economy and reduce dependency on oil revenues. The United Arab Emirates (UAE), characterised by economic diversification and innovative projects, has established itself as a major global trading hub and a finance, tourism, and logistics centre. Qatar's vast natural gas reserves have turned it into the world's largest liquefied natural gas (LNG) exporter, effectively expanding its economic influence. Kuwait boasts a strong financial sector and is a major exporter of petroleum products, contributing to regional economic stability. Bahrain's financial and banking centre attracts businesses and investors due to its business-friendly regulations and strategic location. With its strategic ports and economic partnerships, Oman seeks to transform its economy to reduce dependence on oil and create sustainable growth.

The combination of BRICS+ and the GCC's economic weight establishes a strong foundation for cooperation. The GCC countries, largely dependent on oil exports, seek to diversify their economies and move away from over-reliance on hydrocarbons. Therefore, they are increasingly interested in investing in the vast consumer markets and burgeoning middle class of BRICS+ countries. These economies offer numerous opportunities for GCC countries to diversify their investments and gain access to new markets, industries, and sectors.

Likewise, BRICS+ nations find value in partnering with the GCC. They recognise the Gulf countries' sizable financial resources and expertise in infrastructure development, real estate, and hospitality. This attractive investment landscape encourages BRICS+ countries to explore joint ventures, strategic partnerships, and investment opportunities with the GCC. The GCC's investments in BRICS+ nations can contribute to job creation, infrastructure development, and technological advancements, fostering sustainable economic growth.

Furthermore, the ongoing relationship between BRICS+ and the GCC holds particular significance for the stability and security of the region. Both entities face shared challenges regarding regional security, terrorism threats, and political stability. By enhancing collaboration in security and defence arenas, intelligence sharing, and counterterrorism efforts, BRICS+ and the GCC can contribute to regional stability and peace and eradicate extremist ideologies.

Strategically, the strengthening relationship between BRICS+ and the GCC carries implications beyond their respective regions. Their combined influence challenges the existing global power dynamics, primarily dominated by Western nations. As BRICS+ nations and the GCC continue to assert their economic prowess, they advocate for a more inclusive and representative global governance system. This push for reform in global institutions, such as the United Nations Security Council, aims to ensure a more balanced distribution of power and enable the voices of emerging economies to be heard on matters of global significance.

To strengthen their economic ties, BRICS+ and the GCC have been exploring various avenues for cooperation. Trade relations have been growing steadily, with bilateral trade agreements, preferential trade deals, and efforts to remove barriers to trade and invest- ment. Establishing joint economic committees, business forums, and trade delegations has facilitated dialogue and collaboration between the two sides. In addition, their com- mitment to infrastructure development, connectivity, and sustainable development has opened doors for investments in transportation networks, energy projects, and technol- ogy transfer.

Moreover, energy cooperation between BRICS+ and the GCC holds immense po- tential. The GCC's significant oil and gas reserves can meet the growing energy needs of BRICS+ countries, while BRICS+ economies can offer technological expertise and investment in cleaner energy sources, energy efficiency, and renewable energy projects. Sustainable energy partnerships can contribute to reducing greenhouse gas emissions, combating climate change, and achieving international climate commitments.

In conclusion, the ongoing relationship between BRICS+ and the Gulf Cooperation Council presents vast potential for collaboration and mutually beneficial partnerships. Economic synergies shared security concerns, and the desire for a rebalanced global gov- ernance system motivate both entities to foster stronger ties. By leveraging their economic strength, strategic positioning, and collective influence, BRICS+ and the GCC can shape the future of the global order, advocate for reforms in international institutions, and ultimately contribute to a more balanced and inclusive global governance structure.

46

THE FUTURE OF THE GLOBAL ORDER AND THE ROLE OF BRICS+ AND GULF COUNTRIES

— • —

T he existing global order is undergoing significant transformation, driven by shifting power dynamics and the rise of emerging economies. This chapter delves deeper into the implications of the rising influence of BRICS+ (Brazil, Russia, India, China, South Africa, plus the potential addition of other emerging economies) and the Gulf Cooperation Council (GCC) in shaping the future global order. It explores the economic perspectives, geopolitical implications, strategic convergence between BRICS+ and the GCC, and their potential impact on global governance. The following sections provide a comprehensive analysis of these aspects.

Economic Perspectives: Rise of BRICS+ Countries

The BRICS+ countries, comprising some of the world's most populous and fastest-growing economies, have rapidly emerged as major players in the global economy. Since the term was coined in 2001 by Goldman Sachs economist Jim O'Neill, the BRICS countries have made significant economic growth and development progress.

China, the largest economy among the BRICS, has experienced sustained and robust economic growth over the past few decades, becoming the world's second-largest economy. Many factors, including a large population, a thriving manufacturing sector, and strategic government policies, have driven its economic success. With its youthful demographic advantage and technology-driven services sector, India has also emerged as a major player in the global economy.

Brazil, Russia, and South Africa face unique challenges but have significant economic growth and development potential. Brazil, with its rich natural resources and agricultural prowess, has the potential to become a major global food supplier. With its vast energy reserves and advanced military-industrial complex, Russia has positioned itself as a key player in the energy sector and global arms trade. With its mineral wealth and potential for regional integration, South Africa can be a gateway to the African continent for global investors.

The economic success of the BRICS+ countries has been further bolstered by their efforts to promote regional and global economic integration. Initiatives like the Belt and Road Initiative spearheaded by China and the African Continental Free Trade Area highlight their commitment to enhancing connectivity, trade, and economic cooperation.

Potential Economic and Technological Partnerships with Gulf Countries

The Gulf Cooperation Council (GCC) countries, situated in a region rich in oil and natural gas reserves, have long significantly influenced global energy dynamics. While their economies have traditionally depended on hydrocarbon exports, the GCC countries are now actively working to diversify their economies and reduce their reliance on oil and gas.

The BRICS+ countries have the potential to forge meaningful economic and technological partnerships with the GCC. The complementarities between these entities present numerous opportunities for collaboration. For instance, China's Belt and Road Initiative aligns well with the GCC's vision for infrastructure development in the Middle East and beyond. Investments in renewable energy, information technology, and agriculture sectors can create mutually beneficial partnerships between the BRICS+ and the GCC countries.

Furthermore, the GCC countries possess significant financial resources, which can be leveraged to support the development of the BRICS+ economies. Gulf sovereign wealth funds, such as the Abu Dhabi Investment Authority and the Qatar Investment Authority, have made substantial investments in various sectors globally, including real estate, infrastructure, and technology.

Energy Dynamics: GCC's Role in the Global Order

The GCC's role as a major energy supplier is crucial to the global economy. The region accounts for significant global oil production and holds substantial natural gas reserves. The GCC countries have traditionally been key players in shaping global energy dynamics and maintaining stability in global energy markets.

Saudi Arabia, as the world's largest producer and exporter of oil, has historically played a significant role in setting global oil prices and managing oil supply. Other GCC countries, such as the United Arab Emirates, Qatar, and Kuwait, are major players in global energy markets.

However, the dynamics of global energy supply and demand are changing. The growth of renewable energy sources and increasing environmental concerns have led to a global energy transition. The GCC countries adapt to these changes by investing in renewable energy projects and diversifying their economies. For instance, Saudi Arabia's Vision 2030 aims to reduce the country's dependence on oil revenues by developing new economic sectors and fostering innovation and entrepreneurship.

Geopolitical Implications and Power Shifts

The evolving global order has significant geopolitical implications, particularly about the role of the United States. The rise of emerging powers like the BRICS+ countries and the increasing influence of the GCC challenge the traditional power structures and alliances.

The United States, long considered the dominant global power, faces competition from China economically, politically, and technologically. The BRICS+ countries, with their combined economic might and growing influence in international organisations such as the United Nations and the World Trade Organisation, seek to balance the power dynamics.

The GCC countries, situated in a region of geopolitical significance, actively pursue foreign policy initiatives to balance competing interests. The Saudi-led coalition's intervention in Yemen, Qatar's attempts to diversify its alliances, and the United Arab Emirates' projection of military power in the region are all indicative of the shifting geopolitical landscape.

These power shifts and geopolitical alliance realignments directly impact global governance structures. The influence of emerging powers like the BRICS+ in organisations like the G20 and the BRICS New Development Bank challenges the dominant position of Western powers. Moreover, the GCC's strategic location and economic importance make it a key player in regional and global affairs.

Strategic and Economic Convergence

Strategic and economic convergence between BRICS+ and the GCC holds immense potential for reshaping the global order. This convergence can manifest in various ways, including cooperation in counterterrorism efforts, security cooperation, and infrastructure development.

In counterterrorism, the BRICS+ and the GCC countries face shared challenges in combating extremism and ensuring regional stability. Closer collaboration in intelligence sharing, joint military exercises, and capacity-building initiatives can help address these challenges effectively.

Security cooperation is another area where convergence between the BRICS+ and the GCC countries is possible. Given the increasing complexity of security threats in the region, including tensions in the Persian Gulf, conflicts in the Middle East, and regional rivalries, forging strategic partnerships can enhance stability and facilitate crisis management.

Additionally, infrastructure development presents opportunities for collaboration between BRICS+ and the GCC countries. The GCC's ambitions for large-scale infrastructure projects, such as the Saudi Vision 2030 and the Qatar National Vision 2030, can benefit from the experience, expertise, and investments of the BRICS+ countries. The

Chinese-led Belt and Road Initiative can provide a framework for enhanced connectivity between the GCC and the BRICS+ countries, facilitating trade, investment, and people-to-people exchanges.

Implications for the Global Order

The rising influence of the BRICS+ countries and the GCC has far-reaching implications for the current global order. These emerging powers challenge the existing power structures and provide alternative development and governance models. Western dominance in international institutions like the United Nations and the International Monetary Fund is being questioned, leading to calls for more inclusive and representative global governance.

The growing influence of the BRICS+ countries and the GCC also has regional and global security implications. The multipolar nature of the evolving global order requires effective dialogue and cooperation between major powers to address common challenges such as terrorism, climate change, and nuclear proliferation. Strategic and economic convergence between the BRICS+ and the GCC can contribute to stability and peace globally.

Moreover, the rise of the BRICS+ and the GCC countries presents economic growth and development opportunities for the rest of the world. Their investment in infrastructure projects, innovation, and technology can spur economic activity and create jobs. Increased trade between these regions can lead to greater prosperity and higher living standards for their populations.

However, the changing global order also poses challenges and uncertainties. The rise of new powers can lead to geopolitical rivalries and competition for resources and influence. The potential for power struggles and conflicts cannot be ignored, and global leaders need to navigate these complexities through dialogue and diplomacy.

Furthermore, the actions and policies of the BRICS+ and the GCC countries will affect global governance structures. With their growing influence, these emerging powers can shape the rules and norms of international institutions and challenge the dominance of Western powers. It is crucial for all countries, both established and emerging, to work together and find common ground to address global issues effectively.

Conclusion

The future of the global order is being shaped by the rise of the BRICS+ countries and the increasing influence of the Gulf Cooperation Council. The economic perspectives, geopolitical implications, and strategic convergence between these entities have the potential to reshape global governance structures and power dynamics.

The BRICS+ countries, with their rapid economic growth and commitment to regional and global integration, are emerging as major players in the global economy. With their strategic location and economic importance, the Gulf countries play a crucial role in global energy dynamics and geopolitics. The synergies between the BRICS+ and the GCC present opportunities for economic and technological partnerships that can benefit both regions and contribute to global development.

However, the changing global order also poses challenges and uncertainties. Power struggles, geopolitical rivalries, and conflicts may arise as the balance of power shifts. Global leaders must navigate these complexities through dialogue and cooperation, ensuring a peaceful and prosperous future for all.

In conclusion, the future of the global order and the role of the BRICS+ and the GCC countries are intertwined. Their rising influence will shape global governance structures, economic dynamics, and geopolitical relationships. All countries must work together to find common ground and foster cooperation to address the challenges and opportunities of the evolving global order.

REFERENCES FOR FURTHER READING

— • —

Agnew, John and Corbridge, Stuart (1995) Mastering Space: Hegemony, Territory and International Political Economy. London: Routledge.

Barry Buzan and Ole Waever, Regions and Powers: The Structure of International Security (Cambridge: Cambridge University Press, 2003).

Blanchard, Christopher M. China and the Middle East and North Africa (MENA), Congressional Research Service, August 4, 2023.

Blanchard, Christopher M. Kuwait: Issues for the 118th Congress; Congressional Research Service, Updated July 12, 2023.

Borck, Tobias. Seeking Stability amidst Disorder. Hurst Publishers, 2023.

Brown, Stuart (ed.) (2011) Transnational Transfers and Global Development. London: Palgrave Macmillan.

Burki, S.J. (2011). South Asia in the New World Order: The Role of Regional Cooperation (1st ed.). Routledge.

Christensen, Peer Møller and Li, Xing (2013) "China's Self-perception of its Security Situation: The Nexus of the Internalities and Externalities", Journal of China and International Relations, 1(1): 26–45.

Chun, C.W. (2021). A World without Capitalism? Alternative Discourses, Spaces, and Imaginaries (1st ed.). Routledge.

Colombo, Silvia. Bridging the Gulf: EU-GCC Relations at a Crossroads. Roma: Edizioni Nuova Cultura, 2014.

Cox, Robert W. (1983) "Gramsci, Hegemony and International Relations: An Essay in Method", Millennium: Journal of International Studies, 12(2):

Danny Quah, "The Global Economy's Shifting Centre of Gravity," Global Policy 2(1)(2011).

Dargin, Justin. The Rise of the Global South. World Scientific, 2013.

De Coning, C., Mandrup, T., & Odgaard, L. (Eds.). (2014). The BRICS and Coexistence: An Alternative Vision of World Order (1st ed.). Routledge.

Ekins, P. (1992). A New World Order: Grassroots Movements for Global Change (1st ed.). Routledge.

Elmuradov, A. (2022). Russia and EU in the New World Disorder: Revisiting Sovereignty and Balance of Power in the study of Russian Foreign Policy (1st ed.). Routledge.

Gilpin, Robert (1987) The Political Economy of International Relations.Cambridge: Cambridge University Press.

Gramsci, Antonio (1971) Selections from the Prison Notebooks. Quintin Hoare and Geoffrey Nowell Smith (ed.). London: Lawrence & Wishart.

Huntington, Samuel P. (1993) "The Clash of Civilizations?" Foreign Affairs, 72(3): 22–49.

Jacobson, D. (1994). Old Nations, New World: Conceptions Of World Order (1st ed.). Routledge.

Jürgen Rüland, and Astrid Carrapatoso. Handbook on Global Governance and Regionalism. Edward Elgar Publishing, 2022.

Kennan, George (1976) "Policy Planning study (PPS) 23", Department of State, 24 February 1948. (The complete paper was published in 1976 in Foreign Relations of the United States 1948, Vol. 1, No. 2).

Kiely, Ray. The BRICS, US "Decline" and Global Transformations. Basingstoke,: Palgrave Macmillan, 2015.

Kumar, R., Mehra, M.K., Raman, G.V., & Sundriyal, M. (Eds.). (2022). Locating BRICS in the Global Order: Perspectives from the Global South (1st ed.). Routledge India.

Laidi, Zaki (2011) "The BRICS Against the West?" CERI Strategy Papers, No. 11. Available at http://www.sciencespo.fr/ceri/sites/sciencespo.fr.ceri/les/n11_112011.pdf.

Li, Xing (ed.) (2010) The Rise of China and the Capitalist World Order. Farnham: Ashgate Publisher.

Marek Rewizorski. The European Union and the BRICS. Springer, 2015.

Monyae, David, and Bhaso Ndzendze. The BRICS Order. Springer Nature, 2021.

Niblock, Tim, Degang Sun, Alejandra Galindo, and Gerlach Press Islamic Studies. The Arab States of the Gulf and BRICS: New Strategic Partnerships in Geopolitics and Economics. Berlin Gerlach Press, 2016.

Nugée, John, and Paola Subacchi. The Gulf Region. Chatham House (Formerly Riia), 2008.

Paulo. The BRICS and the Financing Mechanisms They Created. Anthem Press, 2021.

Pridham, B.R. (Ed.). (1988). The Arab Gulf and the Arab World (1st ed.). Routledge.

Puppim, Jose A, and Yijia Jing. International Development Assistance and the BRICS. Springer Nature, 2019.

Ruchir Sharma. Breakout Nations: In Pursuit of the Next Economic Miracles. New York: W.W. Norton & Co, 2012.

Salzman, Rachel S. Russia, BRICS, and the Disruption of Global Order. Washington, DC: Georgetown University Press, 2019.

Sharp, Jeremy M. Bahrain: Issues for U.S. Policy. Updated March 24, 2023; Congressional Research Service.

Sharp, Jeremy M.Oman: Politics, Security, and U.S. Policy. Updated March 2, 2023; Congressional Research Service.

Sharp, Jeremy M. The United Arab Emirates (UAE): Issues for U.S. Policy. Updated September 13, 2023; Congressional Research Service.

Shaw, Timothy M. and Besada, Hany (2014) "New Multilateralisms for Regional Development: Africa Post-201", in Telo, Mario (ed.) Globalisation, Multilateralism, Europe: Towards a Better Global Governance Farnham: Ashgate.

Sim, L.-C., & Fulton, J. (Eds.). (2022). Asian Perceptions of Gulf Security (1st ed.). Routledge.

Solis, Mireya, Stallings, Barbara and Saori, Katada (eds.) (2009) Competitive Regionalism: FTA Diffusion in the Pacific Ri. London: Palgrave Macmillan.

Stancy Correll, Diana. "Trump Questions Need for US to Protect International Shipping in Strait of Hormuz," Military Times, June 24, 2019, https://www.militarytimes.com/news/2019/06/24/trump-questions-need-for-us-to-protect-international-shipping-in-strait-of-hormuz/.

Steen Fryba Christensen, and Li Xing. Emerging Powers, Emerging Markets, Emerging Societies Global Responses. London Palgrave Macmillan UK:Imprint: Palgrave Macmillan, 2016.

Stuenkel, Oliver. The BRICS and the Future of Global Order. London; Lanham (Md): Lexington Books, 2020.

Thussu, D.K., & Nordenstreng, K. (Eds.). (2020). BRICS Media: Reshaping the Global Communication Order? (1st ed.). Routledge.

Walt, Stephen M. (1998) "International Relations: One World, Many Theories", Foreign Policy, 110: 29–46.

Wang, Jisi (ed.) (1995) Civilization and International Politics: Chinese Reviews of Huntington's the Clash of Civilizations Argument [Wenming yu Guoji Zhengzhi: Zhongguo Xuezhe Ping Hengtingdun De Wenming Chongtulun. Shanghai: Shanghai Renmin Publishing House [Shanghai Renmin Chubanshe].

Ward, I. (2003). Justice, Humanity and the New World Order (1st ed.). Routledge.

Xing, L. (2014). The BRICS and Beyond: The International Political Economy of the Emergence of a New World Order (1st ed.). Routledge.

Xu, Yi-chong and Baghat, Gawdat (eds.) (2011) The Political Economy of Sovereign Wealth Fund. London: Palgrave Macmillan.

Xu, Yi-chong (ed.) (2012) The Political Economy of State-Owned Enterprises in China and Indi. London: Palgrave Macmillan.

Yoichi Funabashi, "The Asianization of Asia," Foreign Affairs 72(5) (1993).

Zakaria, Fareed (2011) The Post-American World: Release 2. New York: Norton. Updated and expanded edition.

Zheng, Bijian (2005) "China's 'Peaceful Rise' to Great Power Status", Foreign Affair, 84(5): 18–24.